CAN WE TALK?

G'DAY!

IAN 'WATTO' WATSON

WATTO BOOKS

Watto Books, PO Box 241, Woody Pt QLD 4019, Australia

thechampionsguide.com

ISBN: 978-0-9873788-6-6

Publishing consultancy, editing, illustration and design: Belinda Pollard
Typing and copyediting: Melindie Hunt
Cover signwriting: James Marsh & Chad Polinski, Eternal Signs
Cover art creation: Peter Jendra and James Marsh
Photography: Peter Jendra

Reactions to
Can We Talk?

Can we talk? Well if you ever ask Watto, the answer is yes! And in a day and age of so much talk and so much noise it is often hard to hear the stuff that really matters. But Watto actually talks sense! And his words cut through the theories and waffling and once again land in a place of practicality and good sense. Great relationships come from great communication. If you want to learn practical, real-life grit and honesty from the heart of Watto – this book is a treasure trove of more Gold nuggets. I devoured it in one 3-hour sitting and felt like I'd just been hanging out with the great man himself – encouraged and ready to get back amongst it speaking life and love into those around me! Paul Morrison, West Coast Eagles Chaplain, Shed Happens WA

No other author can inspire the men and women of Australia the way Watto does. He writes from his heart to show men and women how to trust, and find or rekindle love and happiness in their lives! It has helped my family and me become closer and be the 'real deal' with others. Peter Jendra

Watto has the wisdom of experience and age, as well as the integrity of a man who walks his talk. We did some personality training early in our marriage and it was very insightful for understanding and appreciating each other more. If you take on board Watto's tools for better communication, you will spare yourself many years of frustration and heartache and fast track your relationships for success! Paul and Rachel McLaughlin

What the world needs now is...people who listen. In this book, Watto shares what he's learned about having good, open, safe conversations that make a difference. He's learned it through experience and he's lived it. He's worth listening to. Ruth Butler, retired principal, Grace Lutheran College

The heart of *Can We Talk?* is about connecting with others on a deeper level. Watto gives us the tools to dig deeper into the conversations we have with those around us which will also strengthen the relationships we have with those we love. Nick Ottens, farmer and business owner

I often fly between Brisbane and Perth and it can take up to six hours so there is plenty of time for conversation, sitting up the front of a Boeing 737. But is it good/great conversation? Read Watto's new book *Can We Talk?* and I assure you that when you finish your journey you and those you have spent time with will be much better people and truly blessed. Tim Nagel, airline pilot

Ian Watson has suffered me as his accountant for over 35 years. In that period I have learnt that communications is the key to good client relations. The art of listening is paramount to any professional who interfaces with many people in their practices. Jim Bryant, accountant

'Hey, do you need a chat?' As a husband, father of 3 sons and a teacher of 26 years, I have often used this phrase to get a conversation going. Is it just me, or is it harder to get conversations going nowadays? Watto's latest book has given me insight into how to make the most of my chats with my wife, sons and students. As with his other books, he is teaching me in a very Aussie way to be the type of bloke this world seems to want and need! What he has taught me I know I can use to help teach others the beauty of having a real conversation. Russell Modlin, secondary school teacher

Watto's fourth book *Can We Talk?* is potentially his best. It has many gems on how important it is to communicate wisely with our loved ones and what a massive impact this can make to the depth and the joy in these relationships:

- It is more concise and impacting.

- It is written for women as well as for men and can lead to the elimination of anguish, frustration and blockages that get in the way.

- It is centred on wise and loving interaction that bears much fruit.

Wise readers will probably highlight the best bits of advice for them, making notes to keep them on track as they work on overcoming the traps that rob us of rich, rewarding, joyful relationships, particularly in marriage. Dr Fred Gollasch

'shed happens'

Men learn from men,
as iron sharpens iron.
Proverbs 27:17

G'day mate...

www.shednight.com

Seventeen years ago I helped kick off Shed Nights for blokes – not the Sheds where men work with their hands but a different type of Shed that goes like this...

It starts off with a ripper burger at 6:30pm in a safe non-judgemental place where men can hear real-deep gut issues – good, bad, happy or sad – through two or three blokes being interviewed up front. It's held on the first Monday of each month and up to 150 blokes from all walks of life enjoy being together.

Shed Happens as blokes encourage each other as they do the journey of life together. They are more than happy to tell it as it is from the heart, so that others can be helped. Shed is a place where blokes are champions for who they are – not for what they do or what they have. No-one is allowed to preach, but only to tell their own story.

I go to many different places in Australia helping blokes get their Sheds happening. So that's why my book contains references to Shed and the freedom that blokes experience in their emotions, heads, souls and spirits, through being in a safe place to spill their guts and become the real deal.

See you on the shednight.com website or call me on 0412 722 455

Thanks!

To the girl of my dreams, Margaret, for loving into
my heart and helping me write this journey.

To our three champion sons, Haydn, Brendan
and Luke – for bringing joy into our lives.

To my champion editor Belinda Pollard
who had to think like Watto again.

To all you champions in my life and in my Shed.

To the Champion of champions for
breathing love and life into me.

Watto

CONTENTS

CAN WE TALK?

1. Can we talk about … what I'd like you to get from this journey?

TO GET YOU STARTED

No matter what's in your past, the
education you've had, or your age,

after doing this little journey with me I
hope you'll see new horizons.

I hope you'll be able to say, 'I'm OK', whether you
meet the Prime Minister, a lady who sleeps on a
cardboard box under a bridge, a rocket scientist,
a cancer doctor or a primary school student.

Asking, 'Can we talk?' is going to be the easiest, most natural talent that can come alive for you – virtually overnight – once you've accepted the challenge. But you've gotta wanna!

Even though you may have had little or no love and encouragement growing up, we can take up the slack and help you develop this skill. You'll be in a safe, non-judgemental, non-manipulative place where those closest to you every day will enjoy conversations with you in a new and genuine way. You're guaranteed to learn fresh skills for your work or business life and bring out the best in your future conversations (and clinch some great deals).

Who am I, and why can I help you with this?

My name's Ian Watson, but I'm often known as Watto. This is the fourth book I've written in recent years, and at the time of writing, I'm 73. I've been married to Margaret for 52 years, and our sons and daughters-in-law have blessed me with six grand-children – three boys (aged 5, 8 and 20) and three girls (aged 7, 16 and 19). I also have many spiritual sons and daughters and grandchildren all around the nation.

Over the past 17 years, I've met many, many men, all around the country – mainly in Shed Happens get-togethers where thousands of men have expe-rienced the free-dom to learn in a safe, non-judge-mental environ-

ment, listening when other men have been interviewed and told part of their stories.

They've shared the bad, sad, happy and good areas of their lives, that have come from deep down in their hearts – and that have sometimes been sealed up in pain and silence for many years.

I was on ABC Radio a few years ago with two mighty colleagues, with a national radio program that helped listeners open their hearts to be real.

For 30 years I've had a successful business in heavy vehicle driver training. My greatest asset has been an ability to connect with people, and one of my greatest privileges has been the trainer's seat, where I've sat in a truck cabin for 8–10 hours with learner drivers. One-on-one, we've built trust and I've given encouragement. I've had the opportunity to test what you're going to read in this book time after time. Then they've picked up a new truck licence as a bonus!

I've lost count of the number of men's events where I've spoken, mainly about love and encouragement, telling men 'You're OK!'

I know without doubt that the topic of this book is one of the most neglected but most needed things in our country today.

We are consumed by 'the screen' – our mobiles are our best mates, and we have learned to fear having face-to-face conversations. We're texting and tweeting more, and talking less.

If you are in a loving relationship or you want to be in one, the stakes are especially high. **Hearts need a heart connection, not emojis.**

I hope my dream for you comes true, and that **after you've found the treasure in Can we talk? you'll become**

an aggressive listener your friends and family will love and admire.

By 'aggressive', I mean: be involved in the conversation. Be alert, interested, and inquisitive. Think about what they're saying and ask questions. Don't take over, though – the conversation must flow both ways.

You'll be able to let out the magic and quirkiness of your personality and enjoy being the **real** you with those around you. By developing great communication, you'll make better and stronger connections and learn to appreciate each other even more.

Asking 'Can we talk?' opens up hearts, honesty, freedom. It helps people accept themselves as perfectly OK. It makes them brave enough to say, 'I don't know' and 'Can you put it another way, please?'

Once the barriers of mistrust and lack of confidence have been smashed, we're able to begin lifetime friendships and start on the road to work or business success.

Can we talk about … who's Watto?

I started as a happy, fun-loving kid – and I'm the same now, just an old kid! I grew up in a loving family with three sisters, no brothers, and plenty of other family around me.

However, when I was 15, I found my Mum electrocuted – dead on the laundry floor with the washing machine on top of her. When I was 24, my youngest sister Rhonda collapsed and died at 17 from heart failure. **My emotions were smashed and my grief was raw.**

For most of my life I've hidden the fact that I was sexually interfered with by a male relative, **which added anger, resentment and bitterness to the emotional mix inside the usually happy, energetic and enthusiastic kid who was young Ian.**

The best and most beautiful part of growing up was to learn love at first sight when I saw Margaret. She was 15 and a half, and I was 16 and a half. Being with Margaret sure helped me not to focus on the inward pains for a long time, but eventually I had to deal with them.

Yes! I'm free of all the painful past – I'm proof that you can learn forgiveness, and you can overcome grief.

As I write this, our three sons are aged 49, 47 and 44. They have many and varied university degrees. Amongst others, they all have degrees in teaching. All of them can have good, healthy, robust and encouraging conversations – and are great listeners too.

Can we talk? has been going on – not intentionally, and unknowingly – since we gathered every night around our kitchen table. Our conversations might have involved chatting, or counselling, or motivating – but I can't remember anyone ever thumping the table and leaving.

We have learned a lot along the way, and I'd like to share it.

Best moments for me now as a Pop are in passing on these life-transforming skills to my 6 grandchildren. Yes!

They are aged from 5 up to 20, and they are all different, so our talks look different and focus on different things on different days:

- Talking about their hissy fits

- Listening as they say great and challenging words they've read in books

- Encouraging them to speak up about what's on their minds

- Sharing strong views on the things that matter to them, in a safe space

- Having a robust face-to-face on any topic, no matter how hot

- Having adult conversations easily and naturally.

So, can we talk? Sure can, and it works! The gift that's all packaged up in this book is something I want to pass on to my grandchildren especially. I know it will ensure that they will experience joy, living life with their families, friends and workmates.

Can we talk about ... Wattoisms?

I began playing AFL when I was 12, and my sons and grandsons have played football, cricket and basketball – so I often use footy terms to get my point across in day-to-day living.

I also use some 'Wattoisms' that I hope you'll relate to. For instance, I call God the 'Big Fella', and the Bible the 'Work Manual for the Champion Life', as it tells us how to do life.

There comes a time in every life when you look up and say, 'Are you real, Big Fella? Or are you just a fairy tale? Can you show me in my life that it's more than a fluke, good luck or chance? That it's not just in my mind? Let me know that you are real.'

As a young bloke, I kept secretly asking, and the Big Fella kept showing me things that proved that my life was more than ME.

I asked him to teach me to trust him as we went along the journey, especially during the last 17 years since I was diagnosed with prostate cancer. With all the different treatments I have had, I know that he's got me covered. **He blew the first breath into me at the start of my life, and when my time's up, he'll take me home and I'll be with my Mum, Dad and sister in heaven.**

So far no one has shown me a better set of rules for life than the *Work Manual*, so I'll stick to what is tried and proven beyond doubt.

The motivational verses in it I call 'little beauties', or 'gold', or 'little gems'. I put some of them into this book, so anyone who isn't used to the *Work Manual* yet won't feel like I'm making them up.

We've all been given a free will to say yes or no, and it's not my right to judge anyone or try to force my opinion.

It isn't about 'religion' or rules! You don't find satisfaction deep within your heart and soul from chasing rituals, traditions, or stuff that's human-created. You can have all the gear, but you can have no idea!

For me, it's about the Big Fella as the Head Coach. He's showing his way, love and encouragement to all the players in this big world team, and how to have a great life – as I have.

So, settle into your chair, and let's start the journey!

Can we talk about ... love?

Learning to love is really one of the most important things we get the opportunity to do in our life. You don't have to blow it!

Love never fails. That's the real-deal stuff made in heaven.
Remember,
when the power of love
is in absolute control
of the love of power,
then it's going to be fantastic.

Can we:

- listen?

- hear with our hearts?

- be counted on?

- listen without letting our bias get in the road?

- feel OK to contribute to the mix?

- listen without hammering away with our own opinions?

- encourage another person into a safe, non-judgemental conversation?

- let the quirky aspects of our personalities emerge?

- love the unlovable?

- thankfully take in love and encouragement?

- come to grips with asking the Big Fella to help us learn how to trust him?

If you can do these things … you'll dream dreams and find fulfilment. You'll have joy in the heat of battle.

Can we talk about … doing life with the people on the journey with you?

Since I was diagnosed with prostate cancer 17 years ago, I've attended various cancer clinics for different kinds of treatment. It has been an ongoing battle to try to destroy and remove rogue cells before they can attack a bone or another organ.

The nursing staff and the doctors are all amazing, and you couldn't work in that field without a special gift. They speak and work life into you. But I know there are times when they go home at night knowing that they can't come up with any more. How do they cope with that, without dumping on their partner or their children, or hitting the bottle?

I love all the people who work there. They always give their best. 'Judith' looks after the tea, coffee and lunch. She's now retired from her career as a podiatrist but loves people and wants to keep contributing in the community and helping wherever she can.

Can we talk? She's an expert, and uses the right words, and the right number of words – to you and from you. She doesn't need to apologise for anything. She just goes into cruise control and everyone leaves the clinic better off for the coffee and cake or lunch. **It has very little to do with the food, and it's all about her very special gifting. Her natural gift is encouragement.** I hope you don't need to visit a cancer clinic to meet a Judith.

Today, Judith wasn't there. A young 35-ish nurse said, 'I'm the stand in "tea lady" for Judith today, but I know no one can be as good as the beautiful Judith.'

I waited my moment and said, 'I'm Watto. I like black tea, no milk or sugar, and yes, I'd like lunch sandwiches please.' Then I said, 'What's your name?'

She said, 'Carol.'

'Hi, Carol. Thanks for doing one of the most important jobs in this place, because everyone else is looking flat out. My doctor had some hard things to say to Margaret and me today, and then you turn up with that game-breaker, a cuppa tea. This is the first time I've met you. Are you from another clinic?'

'No, I'm surprised we haven't met,' she said.

'Carol, can I give you a word of encouragement? Next person you see, you don't need to apologise for being a stand-in for Judith. **Just be Carol and do your best, like you do when administering the chemo. You'll be so welcomed by all. Remember, Carol – just be the best Carol you can be with the cuppa.**'

She thanked me and said, 'Got it!' She popped her head in twice more to give me a smile, before removing the canula and sending me home.

I hope you can be encouraged by Carol's story, and pass on the encouragement to all the others in your life. Remember, no manipulation, and don't 'fluffy duck' anyone with flattery that is not genuine.

Just plain old encouragement and love if you want to learn about sharing real-deal love with all.

Can we talk? And win!

TO REMEMBER...

Talking is mostly about LISTENING! Be alert, interested and inquisitive.

Look for opportunities to give someone a word of encouragement.

2. Can we talk about ... what makes you, YOU?

It can be easy to confuse personality with character. Character is a vital part of who you are. It's developed from things you've learned. It's affected by people you do life with, the choices you've made, and chances you've taken. It's influenced by your family background, your upbringing, and many more things that you take into your being. It makes up the essential YOU.

My dad, favourite footy coaches, uncles, schoolteachers and a neighbour with no children of his own, but who was really interested in my wellbeing, all added to my character development.

The differ-ence between personality and character is that personality is

Don't confuse personality with character!

what you are born with, the 'face' that everyone sees day in and day out. Character is the deep you – your core being, your spine, your integrity, your foundation.

Since acknowledging the spiritual part of who I am, God, the Big Fella – as my Father – has been the main source of my character development. His Son, Jesus the Bloke, has been helping me make right choices. You might wonder how that could work.

Can we talk? – and I'll show you how it worked for me!

Your **personality** may be described as extrovert or introvert, shy or confident, energetic or relaxed, funny or serious, optimistic or realistic, and more.

Your **character** may be good or bad, strong or weak. Good character shows out in kindness, honesty and integrity, to name a few.

Character shows up from the inside out. Character is what you do, and who you are. Learning what makes you tick, and how you interact with others, can make you a better person – a better lover, parent, and friend. It can help you with your business or your job, your fun times and family times. It can help you meet new people who will enrich your life – and you will enrich theirs.

Who are you when you're on your own and no-one's looking?

Your character never stops changing, and as it develops, you can be attracted to certain people – good or bad – and they will affect you. **It matters who we spend time with, and how we spend our time.** Spending time in good company and with positive people leads to good character. Spending time in low-life company and/or with people who enjoy complaining means you're putting yourself down too.

Do you feed the angry dog, or the happy dog? **Whatever you do will have life-changing consequences, and it can help you – or hurt you –down the track. You reap what you sow!**

It's about choices or chances. It's important to help other people develop if you can, but sometimes you've just got to turn away – or even run away – because it can drag you down too.

I really enjoy being in a group of people who are confident in knowing who they are, who all have different personalities and strong characters, yet who can appreciate each other. They respect one another's strengths and differences, with an awareness of the things that could annoy others. **They are switched on to life.**

This is a group that doesn't shut down, clam up,
have a hissy fit or spit the dummy
when the conversation may introduce a little
tension,
or someone has a different opinion from theirs.
This group can listen to the whole person in you,
and laugh
and get on with life.

People like this are game-makers and innovators. Their creativity just oozes. They're confident and can laugh at themselves. They're great to be with**. These skills can be developed and learned – but you've gotta wanna!**

It can bring out the gold in all of us when we're comfortable with living on the edge and enjoying it. **If, on the other hand, people are on edge and defensive, the conversation can't flow.** We're too cautious in case someone's offended. It's like walking on eggshells, and isn't fun or exciting. In fact, it can be boring when everyone's worried about saying the wrong thing.

How do you come across when people are looking at you? How does your **character** shape up? **Here's a tough question – do people like to be with you, or would they rather give you a wide berth?**

You're OK to be yourself

Know that you're OK. Don't believe anyone who tells you that you're no good. Don't believe any lies.

When we understand ourselves and accept who we are, it is easy for us to join in and to enjoy being with other people much more. We're all unique!

The issue of personality is, and has been, very important for me. When I was growing up, I often felt lonely. It seemed everyone was picking on me and rubbishing me because I was 'out there' all the time and in people's faces. My natural inclination is to have a big opinion on all subjects – and that can get me into trouble!

Once I attended a professional development workshop with 50 other driver trainers. One of the sessions was with a psychologist who guided us through a personality study. After asking us a series of questions he posted up a huge chart with lots of boxes with different descriptive words in each.

The psychologist called all the answers and matched the people in the room with the boxes. Then he asked, 'Anyone left without a box?' and yes! It was me. Everybody else laughed. So I felt like some sort of weirdo.

When I told him my score, I was the only one to match up with the box marked 'Entertainer'. **I had to accept who I was that day and be happy to like myself – as different. It was a defining moment, and it helped me to understand myself better.**

Don't be confused with who you are. You're OK and don't let anyone tell you otherwise. I don't get embarrassed by who I am anymore. Be encouraged – be yourself and like yourself. You have much to contribute.

Understanding the differences helps us

Understanding who you are can make your relationships great, and your love better and better. It can help you succeed at work, help you and others achieve goals more easily, and bring out the best in those doing life with you.

Your personality is the outside, visible part of who you are – what you look like on the outside to others around you. Own your personality, and enjoy who you are.

I wish I'd known sooner about different personalities. It would have helped me understand others better. When I was younger, I might have persisted longer with other people instead of writing them off, calling them losers, or thinking them dull and boring.

I'm telling you a lot about **my extroverted personality** not because it's the best kind, but because learning how I tick made a big difference for me. I want you to get to know just who you are because I reckon **we all need help with this. It is so vital in the world today.**

Your personality most probably won't be like mine. Don't write me off, because I'm not writing you off. Don't push the stop button, just hit 'pause' every now and then and think: *Can we talk?*

Personality tests are great when they help us appreciate another person, but it's very important that we don't label and put each other in a box. You don't want people to think that's the way you are, and that you'll never be any different. Neither does anyone else.

You may have experienced times when someone tried to put you into a box and shut the lid. Or you might have had a negative stamp or brand put on you when you were young. That can leave you bruised and hurting. It's cruel and can hold you back in your development. It can prevent you becoming the real you.

It happens because they don't really understand you, and it can hurt, big time.

It's not because you're no good. It's because they're seeing you through the bias of their own personality. Those tinted glasses they're wearing may not show them the gold in us – or how different we could become. But on the other hand, if there are ways we express our personality that are offensive, we can deal with them by growing in character.

Nobody's perfect – and our personalities are not set in concrete. With the help of the Big Fella the positive side can shine, and the negative part can be transformed into gold.

If we allow God into our spirit we can continually change to become more like his Son, Jesus, who was the most perfectly balanced person who ever walked on the face of the earth. Two thousand years later, he can be our yardstick for a champion life. This is worth spending a little time thinking about. **You can break free and enjoy becoming the person that the Big Fella created you to be.**

The Creator of the universe showed me that his box doesn't have a lid. So don't be boxed in any way, shape or fashion. **Be free to flow!**

The Creator of the universe showed me his box doesn't have lids!

When you come to know what makes you tick, and what makes you different from those around you, it takes away a lot of stress, anxiety and even panic you may have experienced. It can save many arguments – and at times save you from having to give up or give in to someone else's unfair claims.

Can we talk about ... YOU?

If you find you are running into snags with one or two people you care about, have a look at how your emotions play out.

- **There's nothing wrong with them – your emotions are your emotions.** Own them!

- Once you realise how they play out you can address them. Whether good, bad, happy or sad, deal with them. They can be great – and they can hurt. Be courageous with this – it could be costing you a better job or freedom from pain and shame.

- **You can't change other people.** Only they can change themselves.

- **You CAN change yourself.** I know this from personal experience.

- **The really interesting thing is that other people have changed BECAUSE I HAVE CHANGED.** I can guarantee you that this has worked for me!

I asked the Big Fella for help because it's better and deeper and longer lasting. I was desperate to make sure I wasn't going to stuff up with the most important people in my life. No more emotional derails. No more telling myself my 'please feel sorry for me' story.

Keep focused and make it happen – it always works for me. Keep it as simple as possible. The old KISS principle!

I guarantee this will change your life for the better. It can even be financially rewarding – you can do fantastic business deals or get that promotion, because you know how to listen, and how to talk.

We make it happen – with help from the Big Fella. Come on, you can have a crack!

Winners are grinners

Your personality isn't acquired. You don't have to try to get one! It's the natural you that arises out of your emotions and thoughts. I'm still the same personality at 73 as I was when I felt like I was being wrongly judged as a boy (that was my take anyway, 'poor little Watto' – ha-ha).

You are who you are. It took me far too long to understand who I am, and I don't want anyone else to miss out on feeling this freedom.

When you really know how you tick, you learn to see what's going on and how the other person in the conversation feels.

Listen, listen, listen before you speak. You can be more sensitive and always get gold instead of mud in your face. Don't stress. You're OK! You can gain some thinking time to understand where they're coming from. **You choose! It's your call.**

No-one is better than anyone else

Once you really get to know each other, it's about appreciating other people for who they are, and knowing that you're OK. You don't have to fit into anyone else's expectations. I guarantee you will gain confidence in all further talks.

You can show different sides of your personality at different times and places in your life, but usually there are a couple that are more dominant every day.

Don't waste good energy trying to change others. Learn to understand their personality.

Don't get too hung up on this – it ain't rocket science – but the understanding and acceptance of others will ensure a great and happy life together.

Connecting with others is a big winner for everyone and it turns into gold. God made us all different but we're all special in our individual ways – he doesn't make junk!

Understanding personalities helps us at work and at home – everywhere!

I reckon we should be taught about personalities in high school. It would reduce so much tension, stress, worry and anxiety, and stop anyone buckling under and/or wimping out when facing trouble. We could handle tension much better. It would also make meeting new people and dating much more pleasant!

This is especially true in this era of mobile phones – as we look down at the screen instead of making eye contact with others.

One of the things I've learned about Aussies is that we prefer communication one-on-one. When it comes to speaking of heart and soul issues, we're generally very shy and introverted. This can change when we're in a group, or after we've been drinking alcohol!

My wife Margaret and I are like chalk and cheese in our personalities – but we click. We complement each other, we accept each other, we love each other, and we don't try to change each other.

I now know that her peaceful personality needs me to cherish and respect her feelings and show genuine love and belief in her. Otherwise I can hurt the girl I love, and that would be crazy. Most of all, we love each other.

Our three sons are like us in some ways, but very much individuals as well, and we have learned to appreciate each other's differences.

There are numerous family stuff-ups that could have been avoided if people had taken the time to talk and understand each other better. When we know we're OK we can enjoy being able to laugh at ourselves.

For the past 30+ years in my truck driver training business, it's been gold learning to recognise, appreciate and accept different personalities. **It's so great to help bring out the best in someone trying to learn a new skill. I can be encouraging and not get annoyed by someone's different personality.**

I have learned not to rub them up the wrong way and how to enjoy my time teaching and encouraging each student. I'm sure they appreciated the change in my attitude towards them – especially when I stopped raising my voice!

So, just be open to change and to new learning.

At work, get on better with your colleagues and your boss. If you run a business, keep your customers and get the drop-outs from your competitors because you understand people's needs. Business is all about people. Treat them well and they'll come back and bring their mates.

Strengths and weaknesses

All personality types have strengths and weaknesses. No single personality type is better than any other. All have good and bad qualities, and all are needed to make this world a better place.

I have come to believe through my life that whatever your temperament or personality, the Big Fella is the One who has given you the abilities and sensitivities that you possess. He has given you those things for a purpose – that you might faithfully work at developing them and using them to live life his way.

Though our temperaments have been tainted – or enhanced – by the world around us, **God can show you the plan he has for you. His plan is to prosper you, not to stuff you up. It's your call though – he gave us free will, and he doesn't force anything onto us.**

One of my favourite sayings is, 'The leader sets the pace of the game.'

- Think about what you appreciate about personalities. You can have an interesting time thinking about all the types of leaders that you've liked or disliked – political leaders, bosses, workmates, church leaders, Bible characters, schoolteachers you've had, your old footy or netball coach and captain.

- Think about your footy team, your church community or your work environment. Has the personality of your leader been reflected in your overall performance? Think about the leadership there, and how the members or players have responded to different personalities.

- Now think about what's going on around you right now. Who do you admire? **In sport, some players' futures live or die if there's a personality clash between them and their coach. In sport and in life, which leaders can bring out the best in all their players' personalities and forge a winning team?**

The leader sets the pace of the game

After this little journey learning about personality, it'll be a lot easier for you to live with, and love, your partner, mates, family and others – rather than wanting to hate and hurt. **This will stick with you for the whole of your life and will produce gold – so enjoy**!

When all is said and done, the personality that others see represents only a small snapshot of the real-deal person the Big Fella created you to be. So just enjoy your life, with all the people in your life. Make it happen! **YOU** are the maker or breaker of your relationships.

You don't have to change your temperament or your personality. You're OK and once you appreciate the other personality types you have the GOLD. Enjoy!

TO REMEMBER...

What do you look like when no-one's looking? Are you able to look at yourself fair and square in the mirror, without distractions? Are you contented with who you are, and Whose you are?

If so, you're in a healthy spot to recognise your stress, worry, concerns and anxieties. *Can we talk?* – about how to deal with them, and smash them.

If someone tries to put you in a box, remember that the Big Fella's box doesn't have any lid. You can become the person he created you to be.

Character is not about loud or soft, funny or serious, it's about traits like kindness, integrity and trustworthiness. Learning to recognise, appreciate and accept different personalities is gold.

CAN WE TALK?

3. Can we talk about … accepting yourself, and appreciating others?

TO GET YOU STARTED

In our families, marriages, communities, playgrounds and workplaces, it's our life together that brings out our strengths and weaknesses – and our clashes.

So let's have a go at sorting this personality thing out!

Our world is filled with amazing people, and we come in all shapes, colours and sizes, with different likes and dislikes. Together we make up the team of life.

Isolation and loneliness have become present-day killers. **We need other people, whether it's a partner, family members or friends. We can't do life well by ourselves.**

Getting to appreciate each other's differences is easy and very worthwhile, so let's not make hard work of this. Keep it simple. It's been a winner for me in getting on with people, so that's why I'm passing it on to you.

In this chapter we want to gain a better sense of who we are, and how it affects others around us. What we really need is to establish connections with others, beginning with basic communication. **But as the saying goes, 'If it's going to be, it's up to me!'**

Can we talk about ... what makes YOU tick?

Does your personality get you into trouble from time to time, but you can't understand how or why?

When I began teaching blokes to drive a truck, everything was going well. It was exciting. I loved the interaction with people and especially the challenge of getting them through to their licences first go.

But there were some blokes I was having a bit of trouble with. I just couldn't seem to connect with them. My way of trying to motivate them was frustrating for both of us.

The type of bloke I was having trouble with was an introvert. He was sensitive, quiet and didn't like to be rushed. Too many words bored him – he liked to work things out for himself after minimum instructions. You might recognise him as you, or someone you know well.

Yes, you've got it, he's opposite to me!

Knowing how we all tick and learning to appreciate each other's differences makes life so much better. **Being different makes life exciting – but clashes of personalities can create huge dramas with your life partner, at work, in your**

family, teams, clubs or churches. It happens everywhere. We need to work out how to stop it happening.

Margaret saw my dilemma and did some personality research to help me understand and better appreciate my truck-driving students. She found something that identified 4 main personality types. It said we all have a mixture of the 4 personalities, but usually 2 of them are more noticeable. Certain ones can emerge in different situations.

It really helped me, so let me tell you about **Personalities According to Watto!** How do you see yourself? This is what I call the 4 main personalities, in Aussie lingo.

1. **Peaceful and Laidback: 'Stay calm – no stress.'**

2. **Happy Party Person: 'Everybody's my mate. Let's have fun!'**

3. **Attention to Detail: 'Let's do it right.'**

4. **Boss, Leader and Make-it-happen: 'I'll get it done.'**

This helped me to accept all students, and to help them enjoy the training too. Once I understood about different personality types I didn't lose customers at the end of their first lesson, and my business grew rapidly. **I learned to bring out the best in others.**

Margaret and I have learned how to make this work in our marriage too, and we're still going strong. Have a crack!

1. Peacefuls

Peacefuls are calm and like a life **without worry or conflict**. They **don't push themselves forward**, show off or come across as more important than anyone else. They're **great listeners**, and they're good at keeping their thoughts to themselves. They prefer to **let others do all the talking or run things**.

- The Peacefuls I met while giving driving lessons gave me the impression that they didn't even want to be there. They didn't talk much. They kept to themselves and appeared to be in their own world. Compared with my exuberance, their clock seemed to tick so slowly that at times I thought it had stopped. I wondered if they even wanted to be in the truck with me.

- If you know me, you can easily understand why an hour with a Peaceful person may have been pretty ordinary for both of us because **at that time, I couldn't understand why people didn't do things my way.**

- I'm a bloke with a Bossy, Happy personality. Growing up, my personality caused me many a lonely tear and a slightly bruised heart. People generally saw me as over-the-top. I know now that I must have almost driven some poor blokes insane with too many instructions.

Something had to change and that had to be ME!

2. Happys

I learned that without any effort or putting on an act, my personality is Mr Happy – the Entertainer. The more people I have around me, the happier I become. **People don't tire me at all but give me energy.** I have a natural **encouraging, positive and affirming attitude** towards others. **I like to be popular** and I get a little hurt when someone doesn't like me, or I don't feel appreciated.

- I like to make things happen, but I don't worry much about the middle bit of the project. I don't mind how or who does this part, just get it done! And let's try to make it a party along the way – everybody's welcome. That's me!

- What matters most to people like me is having fun with others no matter what they are doing. I don't have to work at this – it just comes naturally.

- **If you're like me and 'out there' most of the time, you are described as an extrovert. Appreciate who you are. We're all OK!**

- Have a little think about others you may know who are also like that. Have you been able to enjoy their company, or have they annoyed you? Have you written them off in the past and missed out on fun and great relationships?

3. Detailers

Another personality type **keeps us on the straight and narrow** path to make it happen. They're **very creative** and enjoy the journey towards **trying to do it better**, trying to be perfect.

- **What matters most for Detailers is to cover all bases correctly.** Don't we all need one of these people in our family or team to get things done well? (It can be tricky if you have several in one family or team!)

- This person is a good balance for my personality type, as **he brings out my best and he makes me think deeper and harder.** But because of the way I do things, I can come across to this person as slack or disorganised.

- How does this one fit with you? It's just good to be comfortable with who you are.

- **It isn't complicated.** We need to appreciate those who like to do everything right. We don't want to smash them by branding them as control freaks.

- They like to do things their way – because they think it's the right way and maybe the only way.

- **If they're determined to be in control, they might smile and give you a nod of agreement, but then just get on with taking over.**

- My personality is OK with a bloke who is in control, because he makes it happen. I can get alongside and get on with what is needed from me in the project. This is because I'm very comfortable in who I am, and it can get even better as we work together and grow in trust with each other.

4. Bosses

Another aspect of my personality shows like this: I can **accept a tough challenge** and at times **appear to be aggressive**. I'm a 'driver', and not just of trucks! I'm a **'make it happen'** man. I'm **ready to solve your problem – even if you didn't ask**!

The big question for this part of my personality is, 'Who's in charge? Let's make it happen.'

- Are you like this? Maybe you can identify others in your circle of family and friends who act this way. Again, this is perfectly normal. **You're OK – don't try to be someone else.**

- When Mr Boss comes out of my mouth, some people cringe if they've only known me as the Party Boy. They can read me the wrong way. **This serious, focused, driven part of my personality may come out looking angry.**

- But I'm not angry. I'm just driven with dominance, passion and emotion to bring in the big guns and go for it and get the gold. I'm not trying to change you – but you may think I am, so it's easy for us to get thrown off course.

- **The way you can hurt this type of person is to show them no appreciation for their efforts.** The nicest thing you can do for me is say, 'I appreciate you.' And because this type of person appears to have it all together they can be seen as not needing anything. It's sad and unjust if they're pushed into isolation and loneliness because their differences aren't understood and appreciated.

- **The truth is that everyone needs encouragement – even those who always appear to be on top of things.** I've never seen anyone go backwards with encouragement!

Your personality will come out naturally. There are a lot of people out there getting unfairly smashed and criticised for just being their natural selves. **Let's lift our game and get the GOLD that we've previously missed.**

At Watto's

My three sons are similar to Margaret and me in some ways but also distinctly different from us and from each other. **All 4 personalities show up in them in different ways at different times – as would be the same in all families**.

It's exciting when you **step back** and see how a family ticks. Don't try to change anyone else – it doesn't work! **You can only change yourself.**

We've always encouraged them to be themselves and try to appreciate each other's strengths and differences, and to enjoy and sometimes laugh at themselves over these differences.

Our sons are married and have children. It is important for the whole family to respect each other. Learning to understand each personality has been gold. Every family member feels loved, respected and included in the wider family. **You've gotta wanna make this happen!**

Notice I have given you **a quick look at 4 personality types** to show you how important it is to appreciate each of our differences. **There are more, but these are a great place to start. No one type is better or worse than another**, but we can rub each other up the wrong way if we're insensitive to how our personalities work.

If you find it hard to know what type of personality you are, there is wonderful stuff that has been done to help you work it out. If you want a little more professional input, or to do an online test to figure out the differences, try searching for '16 personalities' or 'life languages'. That will lead you to different questionnaires to help you figure it out. Some you'll need to buy, and others are free.

Which combination are you? They're all good!

Enjoy the difference!

As my wife Margaret is a **combination of Peaceful and Detailer, she is totally opposite to me**. What matters most for Margaret is that she likes meeting people's needs and caring for them. She also values some alone time, especially while I'm watching the AFL on TV! So how do we get on?

You often hear that opposites attract, and it's been that way for us. Two people like me could never live together! Fancy having two of me in a marriage!

We get along like a house on fire now, but there have been times when we couldn't understand each other or get our act together. Our love for each other has kept us working through our differences. We've had years of practice. Our togetherness has got better and better over our 50+ years.

Let's pause for another moment on personalities – what types are there in your family? Workplace? Sports team?

Can you now accept them for who they are – knowing who you are, and bring out the best in your connection?

TO REMEMBER...

Peaceful and Laidback: 'Stay calm – no stress.'

Happy Party Person: 'Everybody's my mate. Let's party!'

Attention to Detail: 'Let's do it right.'

Boss, Leader and Make-it-happen: 'I'll get it done.'

We're all different, and we're all OK.

If we work out what everyone's good at and respect it, we all win.

CAN WE TALK?

4. Can we talk about … how to have a champion chat?

TO GET YOU STARTED

Text messages, email, voicemail and social media are no substitute for saying, 'Can we talk?' and meeting face to face.

Social media, despite all its great features, also bombards us with the bad, sad and evil – which is destructive.

Despite being a communication tool, it can close off true connection, and lead to World War III for many.

The coffee culture helps us to meet and talk, but it doesn't always work as well for men as women – and might not help at all if you're trying to chat to your children.

- Find a place where you can meet and where you'll both feel comfortable. It could be at home, walking on the beach or in a park, while watching sport, cooking a meal, or doing a hobby you both enjoy.

- Turn your phone off or put it on silent. **Leave it off the table.**

- Sometimes, standing or sitting side-by-side is easiest. Many an important conversation has taken place while going for a drive, or at the kitchen sink while cooking a meal or doing the dishes.

Now that we've got our hearts and heads in the right place, it's time to have some important conversations and build connections with the special people in your life.

- How we talk to each other is so important! In fact, it is a country-changer, because it teaches us how to handle judgement and criticism.

- It will help you love and get on better with your partner, your family, your mates, people at work … and even people you thought you couldn't cope with!

- It will help you to find out what really pushes other people's buttons – so you can avoid pushing them!

When a conversation goes belly-up, it's usually because we've done one of the following two things:

1. We may have said to ourselves, 'Poor me! I don't deserve this. **I'll shut down and get back at the other person by giving them the SILENT treatment.'** It's very frustrating being on the receiving end of that treatment, especially if you're a person who's learned to have it out.

2. **Or, we might have reacted with some form of ANGER.** We've raised our voice, thumped the table, got red in the face, our blood pressure has risen, we've folded our arms, and yelled louder.

Sometimes, we can start in silence then end in anger.

When people feel threatened, they will be defensive if they don't feel safe. They may then mentally file away all the insults and upsets, pushing them down, down deep within into silence – and then one day, they all bubble up when something or someone causes them to blow up.

Silence can also be caused by something else that puts us under the pump – money, sex, work or relationship problems, to name a few. These can consume us in silence, but then we lose it, and blast off at someone. This can happen anywhere, but most often at work or at home, where the fallout from the explosion particularly hurts our nearest and dearest.

Let's sort this out so those we love don't cop it. Ask, 'Can we talk?'

In childhood, we learn to build our defences towards anger or the silent treatment

Think about how you have experienced family life, past and present.

Some families don't often eat meals together, due to working hours or other commitments. Or, they may all be at home, but focused on screens – and not each other.

- When you were a child, if your family was gathered around the dinner table, when and how did you fit into the family conversations?

- **How did you learn to join the conversation? How did you unknowingly defend yourself and survive in your household?**

- When you tried to join in, did you end up quietly withdrawing into yourself, thinking, 'What's the use of me trying to get into the conversation? No-one listens to me, and they're not interested in my opinion.' You may have learned to shut up and be quiet as your defence.

- Did your family make you flare up with a good old touch of anger with statements like, 'You don't know what you're talking about?' Or did words like, 'You're an idiot' cause your steamy emotions to blast back at them as your defence mechanism?

Any of this sound familiar? Did you go into silence or towards anger? Or avoid sitting down together?

What happens in your family now? **How would your children perceive their individual places in your family?** What about relationships with parents, siblings, and other extended family members such as grandparents?

When two people won't talk it out... nothing worse!

Silence isn't always the silent treatment!

Perhaps you were an only child and experienced adult conversations with your parents as a norm, as one of my closest mates did. He's very comfortable in who he is.

Sometimes, others who come from large, noisy families think he needs to change so he can make connections. In a big group, he's just quiet and listens a lot. But one-on-one, he and I can have great connection and conversation.

Maybe your parents were good at conversation, and you had no need to develop any 'getting square' weapons to survive among your siblings. You might have grown up to be a strongly independent person, content with your own company and thoughts. However, if your partner comes from a noisy family, you may need to adjust your conversational styles to help each other.

Dealing with old defences

Here's the good news. **Margaret and I needed to learn to deal with our old defences, but we refused to let them get in the road of beautiful communication and love.**

We both learned a lot – about ourselves and each other, and the importance of connection.

Here's a story about our journey.

Years ago, I won the nod for pre-selection in state politics. All my friends had told me I had the gift of the gab and would make a good politician. I can talk under water!

I thought, 'I can make a difference, I love people, I can solve all the problems, I can change the world.' It was also a way out of an office job that made me feel insignificant. It certainly boosted my ego to be pre-selected!

However, this could have been a disaster in my connection and love with Margaret, and certainly with our future communication.

Here's her reflections on that time in our lives:

Margaret says... Ian had been a member of the party for some time, and obviously they had been impressed by his verbal skills, passion and caring nature. I was quite happy for Ian to be involved as it used up some of that seemingly inexhaustible energy he had.

When Ian told me he'd been nominated I went along with it, thinking it would go no further. Then I realised we were getting into something I hadn't expected.

At a women's fundraising gathering there was much excitement from everyone about the possibility of Ian being elected – everyone except me, that is. I envisioned Ian being out night after night as well as at weekends. He would love it, while I would be trying to manage our teenage boys without the influence and leadership of their father.

I also knew how much he'd get involved with people's problems, and then there'd be the criticisms and disappointments he'd have to handle.

Unlike Ian, I didn't think I'd cope with being a public person and having to attend lots of functions. I became very fearful of what the future could hold for us as a family.

At that time, we hadn't got to the place where we could go to God together for direction. I just mustered up the courage in my own strength to deal Ian a blow by telling him I couldn't go through with it. I felt really bad, but he felt even worse. I only had to face Ian, but he had to tell the party, and deal with the pain, embarrassment and shame of pulling out.

It was a very difficult time. We didn't talk much about it and hoped our bad feelings would just go away. But of course, they didn't.

My ego came down with a thud. Man, did I tell myself a sad poor-little-me story! 'How could Margaret do this to me? How come she let me get in this deep?' I felt as though everyone wiped me like a dirty rag.

We needed to talk! Wow, I'm glad we did!

It was a crucial time in our family life. Looking back, leaving politics was the right and better choice, and I'm glad I realised I needed to make Margaret and our boys my priorities.

If I'd gone into politics, would I have had my Driver Training Centre for thirty years, my water truck business, or my Shed Happens journey of many years? Would I have written 3 books and been privileged to encourage so many blokes on a one-to-one basis?

It was a tough call, and I have no regrets. I learned from the past – but I don't live in it!

Now, I run all my business deals past Margaret, and if she says yes, it happens. I never try to sell her my deal. **I don't think about how I could change her way of thinking, but rather how I can change my own.**

I can now see that taking the big hits of reality adjustments on my ego has led to a much more joyful life. In our prideful moments the Big Fella might challenge us, and when he does, we need to go deeper – even if it doesn't make sense at the time!

Sometimes our Creator needs to bruise our brains with a lot of deep thought, to help us mend our hearts.

Learning to play conversation tennis

Our defences of silence or anger come out when we don't feel safe. What's the solution? Can we talk?

If you've played tennis, you know what it means to have a good rally back and forwards over the net. Rallies work best when both players keep returning the ball over the net and keep the play going. We get in some nice little shots, a few relaxed backhands, a few overheads, and a few lobs, and we never try to put the other player off.

Eventually someone wins the point but only after we've both had the best rallies backwards and forwards. The win never really matters, it's the rally that counts.

We can liken this to good conversation, because we want the communication to keep going – just like a tennis rally.

We may occasionally need to have a 'hard word' and are not afraid to lob one up in the air if needed, but if we trust each other we don't want to play any shifty shots against the other person and knock them out of the conversation.

If, however, you think you can ace the other person with every ball, it's a boring old game. The ball never comes back over the net. No rallies, no game, poor outcome. It's the same with conversations – we need to keep them going until we've got the gold.

Keep tennis in mind when you want to have a safe conversation – keep the ball in play. The person who you enjoy having those rallies or good conversations with will always be looking for another rally, because they know a fair and best outcome will be achieved.

There can be times when the conversation doesn't go anywhere, or it can be difficult. Be aware that you or the other person in the conversation:

- could have a hidden agenda
- could refuse to LISTEN, or listen as a token gesture – you can learn to discern this
- could be shy or scared of saying something wrong
- could be having an 'I'm not good enough, poor me' day

- could ask to hear your very personal story, but then want to do a runner without sharing anything about themselves
- could be acting like an arrogant know it all – it's all about ME, ME, ME
- could be a perfectionist – 'look at me, look how good I am at everything'
- could be an emotional person who cries at the drop of a hat
- could just 'spit it' and shut down on the other person as a weapon
- could tell all their stuff and never ask how the other person is – this is very common
- could find fault with everything that is said
- could delight in dropping big clangers on the other person
- could be patronising
- could belittle the other person – not a nice place to be
- could say, 'I know, I know, I know,' when they don't.

5. Can we talk about … having safe conversations?

Have you ever felt smashed by a conversation, or patronised, or shut out from having a say?

Do you think anyone has ever felt smashed, ignored or sidelined while having a chat with you?

Champion, we can win this!

The 4 key points

Remember these four points:

1. What do I want most out of the situation and conversation?

2. What does the other person want out of this same conversation?

3. How best can we continue to create and maintain the safe, non-judgemental place in this conversation where

we can walk away at the end with the best outcomes for both of us? That's what we're after!

4. Politics, sex and religion can be really touchy areas – and can shut down the conversation after someone makes a biased statement. It gets quiet and people squirm. It takes calm and tact to keep talking, or the topic is shut down.

No-one wants to be in a conversation where someone acts in a superior way, has a hissy fit, or drops a tsunami into every conversation and wipes it out.

An information download of thoughts and feelings can be overwhelming when it's dumped on you. It can be scary or threatening if it's unexpected. We want to bring the other person into a safe place so they'll be good to be around.

Don't spit the dummy! Have a rally with the Big Fella instead and tell him what's happened.

You can also find a practice wall to hit – a trusted friend or counsellor to talk to you about how to move forward.

Sometimes the other person doesn't want to talk. They won't pick up the ball and hit it back to you. They may be hurting, and in deep pain, unable to find the words they need.

Remember, there's always more, and it will come out eventually. Just be patient and say, 'Can we talk?'

Learning how to have safe conversations at Shed Night

Shed Nights have become places where blokes feel safe to spill a bit of their stuff without judgement or shame. They do this in the form of an interview. Beforehand, they will have met with their interviewer to establish the basics of what they want to talk about, and set down any 'no go' limitations on what they're willing to share. The interviewer can then guide the conversation.

'Shed Happens' when the speaker encourages us with his story. **It's his story, and we can't argue with it.** Shed Nights have taught us to be open and speak without fear of being ear-bashed and told that we're idiots, or that our ideas and opinions are hopeless.

It's freeing and very refreshing. For lots of blokes who have felt lonely and isolated, sharing genuine emotional connection can be a new experience. Think of it as like a snake shedding its skin!

Shed is not just a place, but an experience – and when it's from the heart, it has mighty consequences for freedom and healing.

Learning how to create a safe environment and how to have good yarns about matters deep down in our hearts will bring rewards in our relationships. We learn skills at Shed that we can use everywhere else.

We try to put into practice these gems from the *Work Manual*:

- **Confess your sins to each other and pray for each other so that you may be healed. (James 5:16a NLT)** *Watto's version: Spill your guts and pray for each other so you can become the real-deal bloke the Big Fella created you to be.*

- **A soft answer turns away wrath, but a harsh word stirs up anger. The tongue of the wise commends knowledge, but the mouths of fools pour out folly. (Proverbs 15:1-2 ESV)**

- **Whoever diligently seeks good seeks favour, but evil comes to him who searches for it. (Proverbs 11:27 ESV)** *Watto's version: Look for the gold, not the dirt!*

Over time, I'm learning. I refuse to let other comments derail an important conversation. **I've made mistakes of course, but I am committed to ensuring the other person remains confident and able to express his or her opinion without my judgement.**

Put this in your conversational toolkit and you're on the way to striking gold in all parts of your life, especially in love and doing successful business deals. A huge winner in all ways for us!

Taking Shed Night home with us

After we've learned the benefits of being able to share good, open, non-judgemental chats, we can take this approach into our marriages, families and workplaces and spread the encouragement.

At Shed Happens, we men must feel safe to speak and not feel judged. But remember, Shed is not just a building – it's about 'shedding' the stuff in our hearts.

- **Talking and listening at Shed can sometimes stir up painful memories and remind us of hurts from long ago. We can't leave those hurtful things at Shed.** We take them back with us into our homes, workplaces, and especially into our relationships with the ones closest to us. We need to sort them out.

- **No more SILENCE or YELLING (being defensive). We men can now deal with the tough moments in our conversations and get on with life as a winner.** The benefits of being open and free to speak and listen safely takes our love into another place.

- **Take care though.** Don't go home and drop a bombshell on your partner, Mum, Dad, brother or sister from something that has come out at Shed Happens. If you've been living with it for 20 to 30 years, it may take more than 5 minutes to sort out.

- **Check the conversation you wish to take home first with a trusted and close friend.** Then tread gently so that both parties feel safe. Our families are being torn apart because of our inability to talk fairly through the tough parts.

Know this my beloved brothers:
let every person be
quick to hear,
slow to speak,
slow to anger. (James 1:19 ESV)

Can we talk about ... safe conversations at work?

As you develop skills in having winning chats, you'll find they also work brilliantly in your business deals, even difficult ones. Once you may have lost the deal; now you can be a winner.

Wouldn't you prefer to face people and safely listen to and engage with them, to find the gold that's within? Those conversations you missed out on before can become some of your best in the future.

Once you've identified your own personality characteristics and understood how you tick, it will be easier to understand how to communicate with other people.

You'll learn how to gauge that point at which you used to walk away – because it was a hot topic, or because there was tension in the air, or because you disagreed with someone else's opinion. With this new awareness you'll be able to hold your ground and create a safe place for both parties – and ask, 'Can we talk?'

All these issues can be much more serious where your partner's concerned, so take care. Emotion can heat the whole thing up without you realising it. Ask God to help you speak without emotion smashing good and safe connection.

You don't need to feel pressured, squashed or shut down

Some years ago, I was upgraded from a local footy coach to a State Coach. **The Director of Coaching at the time saw something in me and pounded me to a higher standard. At no time did I feel unsafe in our conversations.**

Though he gave me a bit of an ear-bashing, he never smashed me. I knew his motives were always heart-driven and had good intent. I was constantly stretched – but I wanted to spend time with him because he was real and genuine, and I wanted to listen and learn. No pain, no gain – it was worth it.

He taught me how to trust his words and intentions, and as my trust grew and I learned not to get rattled, the real-deal coach in me began to emerge.

On the other hand, at another time, I had an issue with a player on my work team.

Everything was rolling along great guns. One day, I over-organised a situation and our communication was severely dented, with the result that he didn't feel safe with me. A few days later he let blast with a 21-gun salute!

In my earlier life, I would have just wiped him. 'I'm the boss, how dare you speak to me like that!'

This time I could allow him to be safe and let it all come out, even though it bruised my pride. I could do this because I'd learned to say, 'Can we talk?'

I thanked him for his courage in telling me, kept my remarks as brief as possible and apologised for where he thought I'd let him down, sticking to the point and not reopening the original pain. KISS – 'keep it simple, stupid!'

A few days later, he quietly and humbly apologised, and I forgave him. I meant it and left it at that – no patronising. Six months on, our understanding and trust for each other had reached a new level, and we did great work together – on a better playing field.

From that day on our communication was more precise, more respectful and more understanding. He was in a better place, and able do his work better.

- I've learned to be more careful in my communication, and think more before I say, 'Can we talk?'

- While I hadn't been trying to bring him down with what I said, how he interpreted it could have destroyed a good relationship. At one time it looked like we had both lost the fight, but today I can tell you we won the war and developed a great business relationship.

But if I hadn't learned how to talk to him, this would not have been possible. I could change myself, but not him.

Can we talk about ... safe conversations with a mate?

One of my closest mates and I have been practising being safe in conversations, usually with heat and tension, for over 50 years. We've proven time and again that we never go past the safe place, because our mateship is the most important thing.

Our differences of opinion regarding politics and footy teams help us both see a bigger and brighter picture. We learn plenty!

People don't usually change their core beliefs – but if we listen, we can certainly learn from each other.

People aren't sausages!

Unlike sausages coming out of a butcher's mincing machine, people aren't sausages – they're not all the same.

We need to learn about their differences, how they like to be treated, what will upset them, and how to encourage them.

Sometimes we need to discern an appropriate point when we should persevere, and when to leave them alone. They may need just a little more conversation or encouragement – or they might need time to think about things you've discussed. If so, don't push – you might push them too far.

This is crucial for everyone. Just keep the lines of communication open!

Let the music come out of you

I've come to identify the moments in conversations when I have a choice to make. I'm better at keeping on track, not retreating into **SILENCE** or dragging the other person into the 'poor-me club', or becoming **ANGRY** and yelling back louder.

Going into silence or anger is like sipping your own poison, and it's going to get you in the end.

If I want the best conversation, it's up to me to work on it. It's important at the start of a conversation to have these questions in mind:

- **What do I want from this chat?**
- **What do I think the other person wants out of this conversation?**
- **How can we stay safe in this conversation and get the best results for both of us?**

The Gold that comes from real-deal champion chats

The Big Fella showed me that at any moment in conversation I can call upon his Spirit in my heart and soul to

guide my speech and motives, and guide me towards the best outcome.

Sometimes this might mean being silent – but not for selfish reasons. Keep it open and free, and the other person will hear your heart in your silence.

Learning to ask for the Big Fella's help hasn't been easy, but the world doesn't know how to help with this. Asking him works for me, but the issue of me trusting God was a challenge at first.

As I've chosen to ask God to be the guide of my life, heart and soul, his Spirit is within me and I learned that I don't need to do this battle in my own strength.

It's up to you if you want to develop spiritually. Just ask the Big Fella!

He guides us to better outcomes. He gives me a peace and satisfaction that keeps me on track in conversation. He picks me up, dusts me down, restores my soul and encourages me back into the battle of life again.

The *Work Manual* says that all things work together for good for those who love the Big Fella (Romans 8:28). It works and God's got me covered. I've learned to trust him, and I try to include him in every chat. As the saying goes, inch-by-inch is a cinch; yard-by-yard is too hard.

If, and when you choose to go with the spiritual part of you, you'll have spiritual discernment within you from God's Spirit. It's another winning promise.

Here's a gem from the *Work Manual* worth a bit of good thinking time:

'The natural person does not accept the things of the Spirit of God, for they are folly to him, and he is not able to understand them because they are spiritually discerned. The spiritual person judges all things, but is himself to be judged by no-one.' (1 Corinthians 2:14–15 ESV)

How I understand this: If we deny the spiritual part of who we are because we think it's hogwash, we miss God's Spirit within our own. Without God's Spirit our head rules our thoughts and actions, thinking the same-old-same-old, and missing the gold. But with the Big Fella's Spirit working within us, we can begin to understand his ways. Then problems and challenges with people and situations become clearer and bring exciting times with winning outcomes.

Summing up – Can we talk?

Can you see how any of your loved ones might be being smashed or shut down by poor conversations or the silent treatment? They think they can't have a fair chat with you. They might feel that you don't accept them, and they don't feel safe.

Now you can invite them back into the conversation by asking them to put it another way, helping the other person to regain trust in you, asking them, 'Can we talk?'

- Great chats can lead to healing in a relationship.

- They lead to more real-deal loving.

- Loving relationships affect others.

- Starting in our homes, one relationship at a time, we can help change our whole nation from judgement and criticism to encouragement and empowerment and God's love!

In understanding the importance of real-deal chats, and making them work in your closest relationships, you will see the amazing transformation from smashed conversations to positive and winning results.

It's easy to extend this into group discussions and team-building conversations. All players can feel safe and welcome to participate. You can help avoid dictatorial comments by people who say, 'This is the way. If you don't like it – the highway.'

Ask the question, 'Can we talk about this?', and listen, listen, listen – and win!

Everyone has something to bring to the mix or project. If we don't get them involved, we can miss out on new and fresh ideas, and the best outcome – and sometimes miss out on making the cash!

One of my favourite movies is *The Horse Whisperer*. It's about a wounded horse, crazed with fear and pain. It needed time to calm down, so that someone could get close enough to draw it towards treatment and healing. The 'whisperer' needed to give the damaged horse space until he'd gained its trust. Eventually it came close to him and allowed him to help it back to health. **Trust overcomes fear.**

Sometimes it's like that with people who are traumatised. They can be full of anxiety and don't even realise it. We need to allow time for trust to build. This works for men and women, boys and girls, just the same. When they feel safe and welcome, they can come back into the communication and you can both go forward.

You may have thought you'd lost the fight, but you can win the war. Let your performance do the talking, and don't tell them – show them! You'll never, never know until you have a go!

TO REMEMBER...

- **Ask the question, 'Can we talk?' and really listen. Ensure both parties feel safe, some of the best outcomes will be gained.**

- **The silent treatment doesn't win love, or successful business deals, and neither does yelling.**

- **We learn our defences in childhood – but we can change!**

- Conversation tennis – play fair! Champion chats are safe chats.
- Are you like the Horse Whisperer or the Horse?

CAN WE
TALK?

6. Can we talk about … the people close to you?

TO GET YOU STARTED

Can we talk about … YOUR RELATIONSHIPS? How to have conversations with the special people in your life – the ones that easily stir your emotions.

So how do your relationships measure up?

With champion chats, it's winnable!

Can we talk about … YOUR RELATIONSHIPS? How to have conversations with the special people in your life – the ones that easily stir your emotions.

So how do your relationships measure up? If you haven't been listening to the feelings of your partner, children, mates, or business colleagues, and want to know what matters most to them each day, here's something you could try.

A great question to ask is, **'What things matter most to you today?'** This can be one of the most important things you will say each day. It can be when you get the gold.

Your two big ears are for listening!

- **LISTEN. Don't try to fix anything instantly, just LISTEN!**

- Don't rush, and **don't have an agenda.** Listen hard to the answer. If necessary, jot it down. Then get on with trying to help in those areas.

- Don't forget to ask gently. You might be able to follow up with either a call or text through the day. If it works better, ask the night before what's important for the next day. Do it mainly to listen, show appreciation and give encouragement.

- You can teach each other how to get the best out of this. It's gold. They'll get it sooner or later and start asking you what matters most for you. Then be ready, because the gold starts to rush.

You can start changing your relationship overnight.

- No more just back and forward, discussing the problem over and over, getting nowhere. Get past it.

- Make it happen. Have fun! Ask the question! Can we talk?

- Listen to each other's feelings. They might be good or bad – but aren't right or wrong. Accept them for what they are – and get on with it.

The solution won't be far off.

> If you take up this challenge for 30 days,
> you'll find it's worth it big time.
> Don't expect them to do the same for you.
> But if you can hang in there
> I reckon you will have well and truly got the picture.
>
> I'm sure you'll be pleasantly surprised
> with heaps of gold at the end
> and find that it's a big winner!

This can change a good relationship into a great love relationship. Love conquers all! Or, as the Beatles sang, 'All you need is love'.

Can we talk about ... you and your partner?

The more Margaret and I have understood how each other ticked, the more it has helped us to LOVE AND ACCEPT EACH OTHER and to stop thinking that our own way was the right and only way.

Her personality is a mix of Peaceful and Detailer. Margaret really values harmonious relationships. She has lots of friends and is calm and collected (unless under pressure).

Living with me in the early years of our marriage must have been like living with a travelling circus for Margaret. I was all over the shop! But she loved me and was determined to make our marriage work. Maybe I'm still like a circus at times, just older and slower! But that's me, and I'm OK – and so are you.

Even though we were and still are very different, we complement each other. I'm sure there are many couples who don't have a clue about different personalities and wonder why they clash so often. **It's tragic and crazy to think that if they had some basic understanding of personality differences, they could have kept beautiful love flowing instead of going.**

Go after the gold, learn to understand our differences, and put the knowledge into practice. You don't need to run away when you come across someone with a completely different personality or temperament to yours. You can stand tall. This also goes for business deals.

> **A long time ago, Margaret and I had inside jobs done on our hearts by our Father God so that they could be open and free, and that has made all the difference to us.**

What about this little beauty – it's one of my favourites from the *Work Manual*!

> **Ezekiel 36:26 says, 'I will give you a new heart and put a new spirit within you; I will remove from you your heart of stone and give you a heart of flesh.' (NIV)**
>
> **This can work for you too. Just go straight to the top and have a serious talk to the Big Fella.**

It's quite likely that in the normal course of your love relationship there will be at least one serious blow-up in conversation – but hopefully not too many more in the future.

Let's nail this. No-one sets out to fall out in a business deal, or in a conversation with their loved one.

- **The main destroyer of love conversations is how we argue. We can't talk fairly! We need to learn how to deal with our emotions,** because the last thing we want is a fall-out with our business partner or lover. We want it to be even better.

- We need to trust, and to ensure that our love conversations build great and strong, long-lasting relationships.

- If we don't, mud-slinging, insults and criticism, or using the silent treatment on each other, can take over.

- This can be soul-destroying. It can send us towards anxiety, depression, loneliness, disturbed sleep and many other body, mind and spirit illnesses.

- We might need professional medical help – and if we think that's the case, we shouldn't delay in asking for assistance. When we're feeling better, we'll be better able to forge ahead in building our relationships.

Good news! **These days Margaret and I get on like a Rolls Royce in cruise control overdrive, and it can work for you just the same.** You've just gotta wanna!

Can we talk about … some tips from Ian and Margaret?

In our marriage, **Margaret and I have come to put into practice the following valuable tips that we hope will help you.** They can be winners in all relationships, not just marriage.

- There will be plenty of times when you'll have to consider ways to bring the other person into the safe place of conversation.

- You may have to rephrase your point. Say it in a different way. You may have to recreate the picture in a more sensitive way.

- You may have to say sorry for being too pushy in the conversation.

- You may have to back off.

- You may have to re-welcome the other person to tell you how they are hearing your point. You then may have to reconsider your approach again.

- You may need to walk away and come back to it another day.

- You may have to accept that the other person does not want anything out of the conversation. It's OK – then you just stop.

- When it involves someone close, you may have to just shut up and listen, and not get cut up because they don't show interest in something that is important to you.

- Just continue to invest love and encouragement into the other person. It will come back to you one day. We reap what we sow.

More wise words from the *Work Manual*:

Whoever restrains his words has knowledge,
and he who has a cool spirit
is a man of understanding.
(Proverbs 17:27 ESV)

How good is this?

Remember, it is not in any way manipulative. Most people will shut down if they are feeling manipulated, used or abused.

This point is worth repeating – no manipulation!

Who's in charge?

You might be the tough one in your home or workplace, and those around you might have more gentle natures. Or maybe it's the reverse.

Gentleness doesn't mean weakness.

If your personality mix works best for you this way, accept that it's perfectly OK for either of you to make the tough calls. Sometimes the balance can change in altered circumstances, such as when the 'tougher' partner is ill or injured.

Think about when you're on a journey. If you're on a plane, the flight crew is made up of people with different positions and skills. If the pilot has a heart attack, you'll be relying on the copilot and flight engineer to land the plane safely. If a crisis occurs, you're all in it together – and you'll be following the instructions of the whole crew.

A rally driver needs a navigator, and a long-distance coach driver can only drive so far before his log book shows that it's time to hand over the keys to another driver.

> **Just be aware of what matters most for each of you in your home or workplace each day, and act on that.**

What's this got to do with better relationships? It may sound a bit crazy, but it all gets down to working out what matters most for each person involved.

When the power of love overrules the love of power, we'll start kicking goals and getting the gold.

If you want your relationships and your life to be great, you can't play power games. They just get in the way.

I'm going to repeat this because it's so important – **when the power of love overrules the love of power, we'll start kicking goals and getting the gold. This goes for the workplace, as well as for families.**

Understanding personalities helps you be a better father

As a young father, before I appreciated anything about personalities, I was more about 'just do it my way', or I'd start yelling.

Our ponies Roughnut and Pawpaw were pretty placid.

One of our sons rode them bareback, yelling and screaming like he was in the Wild West.

Another was not like that, but I just put him on and yelled at the pony to get it galloping. I scared my son, and today it would be called bullying. He probably wouldn't ever get back on a horse again. **I did what I thought was best, and nobody told me otherwise – but it was wrong.**

I treated him the same as his brother, and it was painful for him. The same thing happened when I was teaching them to surf – the boogie board, the surf ski and surfboard.

If I'd known what I do now about personalities, I would have been more understanding about the differences between our sons. It could have been much better for everyone, instead of me yelling instructions like I was back doing Army Basic Training.

I've asked for forgiveness, and we can laugh about it now. Back then it caused pain and stress because I didn't consider each son differently.

My three champion sons are all unique and respond to different kinds of attention and encouragement, and they've learned the importance of connecting differently with their own children.

If you are a parent, have a very serious look at this. Understanding your personality and the personalities of your children can make a big difference.

You may be a perfectionist who likes to follow up on details, for example, and your son or daughter might have a bossy, leader-type personality. You may think you are helping them by talking them down, only to find out too late that you have been firing them up and making them angry or that you've sent them into silence.

You can also drive them away and they can turn towards unsavoury things to cover their pain.

A parent with a dominant personality can send a quiet, shy, introverted child into fear. The parent may not even realise this is happening. **The child can take this fear into later life and have big emotional dramas.**

> Your children may never feel appreciated for their
> natural abilities and strengths,
> because they don't fit into your box.
> You may be frustrating them –
> and neither of you can understand why.
>
> Understand how you – and they – tick, and it
> doesn't have to happen.
> You can sort this out – but you've got to work at it!
>
> Learn what areas of their lives are important to
> them.
> Then you can share their special interests
> and add new depths to your relationship.

If this speaks to you, ask, 'Can we talk?' Apologise to your son or daughter, face to face. Don't water it down.

Explain that you're now coming to understand how they tick and that you're also understanding yourself better. Then enjoy a new and equal connection. You can change and set your child free at any age.

Safe conversations with our children and grandchildren

It's vital that we teach our children to speak to others so that they don't grow up feeling like idiots or second-class. I reckon this has been a greatly neglected area in the past but hopefully things are changing.

I have the pleasure of watching our sons and their wives communicate as loving parents with our grandchildren. I've seen and heard how they speak with their children at their different ages and stages, teaching them how to express their opinions and so learning how to get and keep the communication going in their families.

What if you don't have children or grandchildren?

You might not have youngsters in your life at present. But the Big Fella will put them across your life, and you can build wonderful safe, spiritual relationships with them.

Children learn from people of different generations. Parents receive support and wisdom from older people, who can fill the empty spaces in their lives. Everyone has opportunities for sharing friendship and love. But you've gotta wanna!

Many aged care villages are developing relationships with kindergartens, childcare centres and schools.

Whatever your age, everyone can win.

TO REMEMBER...

Ask, 'What things matter most to you today?' Try doing this every day for 30 days, and see what happens.

Don't try to fix anything – just LISTEN!

No manipulation!

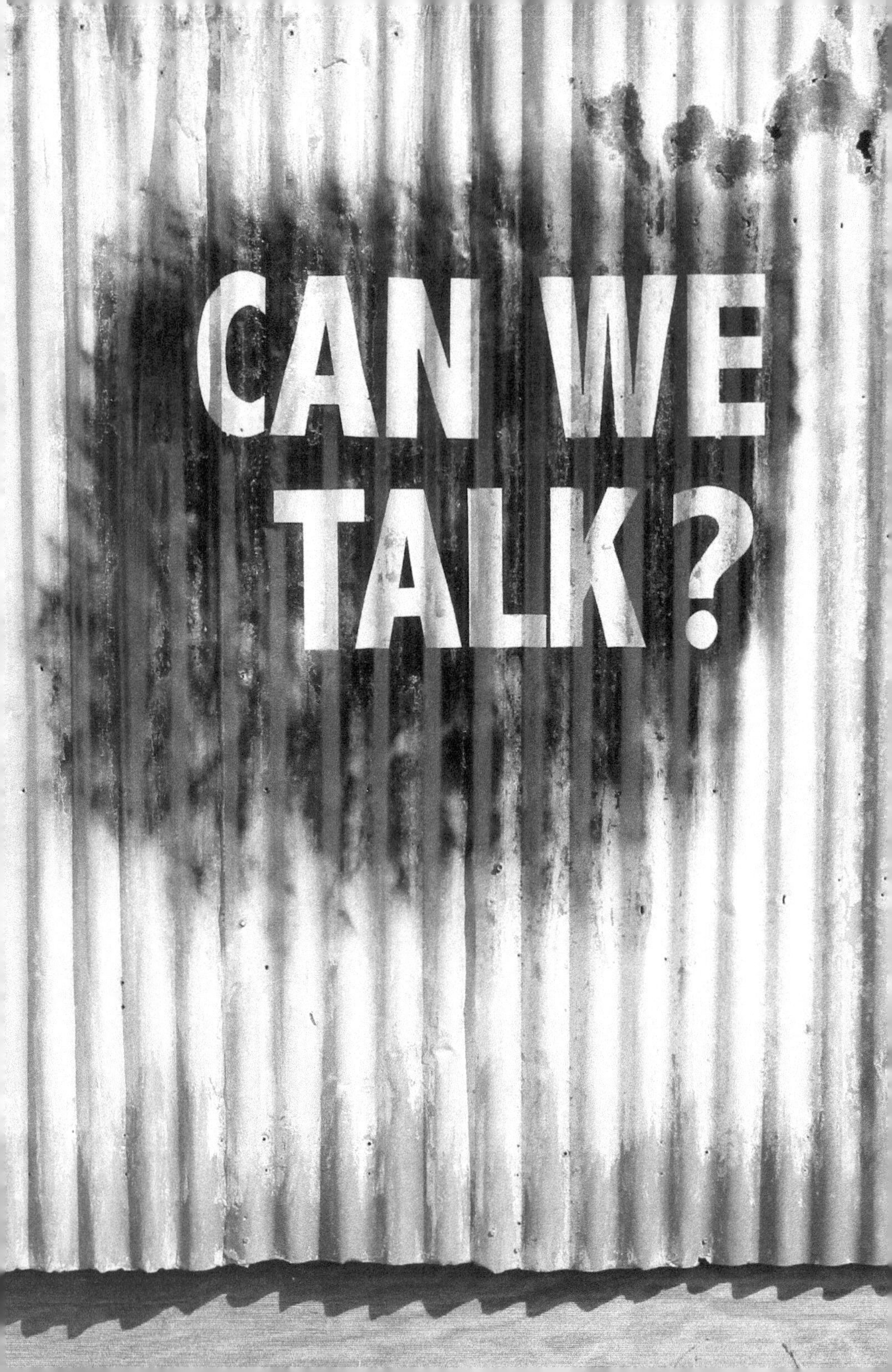
CAN WE
TALK?

7. Can we talk about ... how the best chats come from the heart?

TO GET YOU STARTED

Was your home a safe place for you to express your opinion with plenty of encouragement, laughter and good conversation between your parents? Or was it a place where you were told to be seen and not heard, and to speak only when you're spoken to?

This can help you understand why stuff can come between you and others.

We can fix this. Conversation skills are learnable!

The Big Fella has shown me in my life that there's heaps more gold. He has shown me how to act in conversations with others, especially with Margaret, our three sons, our employees, and even people who don't agree with my comments on politics, my denominational views, my favourite footy team or other hot topics!

He has helped me to listen and has ensured that I have greater respect for other people and their opinions. I keep on learning, and keep chatting, to get this gold. Ask questions, and listen, listen, listen.

All our conversations could be good and healthy if we got through the layers of nothingness to delve into the nitty gritty. Layers and layers and layers – just like an onion. You just keep peeling away.

The nothing zone

Many of us, especially blokes, don't get past the first layer.

'G'day mate. How're you going?'

'OK.'

'What's happening?'

'Nothing.'

We can just stay in the nothing zone forever. Boring, boring, boring! Let's get in close with the ones closest to us – wives, fathers, mates, children, workmates – and learn to have a fair dinkum chat with them.

Don't hold back from the ones you love and live with every day. Don't be scared. Ask, 'Can we talk?' – and be prepared to listen.

You can go a lifetime without ever having a deep and meaningful conversation with someone you care about, because one person makes all the calls and the other goes along with the decision without ever expressing an opinion.

A one-sided relationship can easily end in disaster. For the subservient partner, it's like walking on eggshells. They continually feel anxious, worrying about what is being left unsaid.

This can happen in the workplace too, and leads to stress, misunderstandings, resignations, and high staff turnover. In our journey analogy, it's a car crash or shipwreck that will inevitably happen.

We can just surmise what's going on, but often we're wrong. We end up with the cold shoulder or a bit of fireworks, name-calling or mud-slinging, just because we've let slip some words in carelessness, haste or unintended anger. I'm sure I'm not alone in this!

This can be like sipping our own poison. If it keeps going, one day we have killed a relationship with the one we love or those at work. Let's get back into gear while we are able, or we may be shooting poisoned arrows without even realising!

We can be hurting each other because of our learned communication styles. We don't even realise what's happening, and things can turn out exactly the opposite of what we want. We may not have known another way – but these skills can be learned. **The gold in this book can teach you to have great conversations and change your work and love life forever.**

Be bold and ask the question, 'Can we talk?'

How some blokes from Shed learned to say, 'Can we talk?'

Maurice and his wife have worked on changing the communication style he learned as a child. Here's the story of how they did it:

Slowly I began to realise that I didn't talk enough to my partner. I knew her story – I knew she had come from an abusive relationship. But to be honest we didn't really know each other. Not the real person.

So, we started to talk and talk and talk. We peeled the layers away. **We revealed our deepest layers to each other, bared our souls to each other, took the risk and trusted each other.**

We started looking toward God and put our faith in him. *It helped to do this with the unseen 'Counsellor' there with us.*

This was not quick – it took years.

Communication is a word that scares most people. It is one of the most important things there is, because words have real power over people.

As a parent, you have the opportunity to control the words that are projected into your child's life. *My father didn't want me. The problem with being* *unwanted is that you are treated as a lesser member of the family. You feel dead inside.*

I have gone to extreme lengths to keep the words placed into my kids as positive as I can. *My wife and I have a banned-word list. It includes words like dumb, stupid, idiot, moron, useless, dopey, imbecile, hopeless, worthless. These words have destructive power when aimed at our kids.*

We have 8 kids and are proud of all of them. *All we ask is that they do their best each and every day. Even when they do the wrong thing and we rouse on them, when the lecture ends and the punishment is dished out, the last thing we do is encourage them.* **We leave them with positive reinforcement of a better and brighter future, one filled with love.**

Gordon found a new way too.

I had the unique opportunity of another chance with my first wife, 10 years after our divorce. In the meantime, I had crashed two other relationships before coming back to the first one.

Even though it seemed like a fairy tale, the reality turned out to be far more difficult. But there was something there that we both wanted to pursue that wasn't there before. I think it was something called maturity.

We were very careful about ensuring that, as we grew in our relationship, we checked and double checked with each other that we talked a lot about everything – *to make sure that we didn't end up with a fairy tale relationship that was destined for failure again.*

We worked through each of our issues, but always with the goal of looking to see how the relationship could grow stronger – not building up ammunition to then fire back against each other.

This was extremely hard, because all the issues we both had with each other 10 years before were still there. But now we were tackling these issues together, not man tackling woman.

It didn't get all soppy. **It was an adult journey, of really understanding each other, and being mindful of each other's needs.**

It meant stepping up as a man to treat her properly, to be the head (spiritual covering) of the family, which meant treating her with the respect that she deserved.

It meant thinking outside of myself and thinking about her needs and desires. I had to grow up.

We approached loving each other with much more mature heads. **We forced each other to talk openly**

and fully about every little thing that was going on for us.

On one hand, it seemed a little petty that we would talk about every little thing. On the other hand, we knew so much more about what the other person really liked and didn't like. The pettiness became less as our trust for each other grew stronger – which is still ongoing.

Wayne had the courage to ask another bloke to help him.

I challenged a young man to help me with recognising my anger, as I had become angry in the eyes of my wife and some of my family. He helped me see how the way I made some comments or shared my opinion could shut down a conversation, making it unsafe for the other person to continue. Becoming more interested in finding out more about the thoughts of the other person has helped me more safely share my thoughts and keep the conversation on the table. Less of me, more of others – simple!

The heart of the problem is the problem of the heart

The Work Manual says 'the mouth speaks what the heart is full of' (Luke 6:45 NIV). What hits the heart also hits the mouth. **If there's rubbish and hardness in your heart that's what will come out of your lips – in bucketloads.**

In the spiritual part of who I am, I've learned to ask the Big Fella to show me in my heart and mind what caused me to raise my voice, and how I need to address things.

As we've said before – but it's worth repeating – the *Work Manual* promises, **'I will give you a new heart and put a new spirit within you; I will remove from you your heart of stone and give you a heart of flesh' (Ezekiel 36:26 NIV). If you want this promise, you have to ask – no one else can do this for you!**

This is the proven, winning promise I hold on to. I can assure you that it works for me. Have a red-hot look at it.

The consequences of miscommunication with your partner – or any of your other relationships – can spell disaster, and they don't have to happen.

Let's get this right, here and now, in all aspects of your life – especially your marriage, family and workplace.

The heart of the problem is the problem of the heart!

The better the conversations, the better life gets! Winners are grinners!

Can we talk about ... is it them or is it you?

I enjoy people and find it easy to have a chat with just about everyone who comes across my path. That's how the Big Fella gifted me. I'd even talk to the lamp post if necessary.

Ha-ha! I love people and I'm always looking for ways to give encouragement and love. If necessary, turn the volume knob up!

But even for me, there were a few people who really pushed my buttons and I'd want to strike back. I had to change my ways and I knew that I was the only one who could do it. I had to make this happen.

My little old emotions would light up and I certainly wasn't at the top of my game. I could even shed a tear thinking, 'Woe is me!' **When I allowed it, I was smashed by my emotions and had to learn why.**

I realised that I had a common thing that happened every time. I'd blow up and feel sorry for myself and tell myself a little sad story like, 'Ian, how dare that person say those things or treat you like this, after all you've done for them! You don't deserve that. They should show you more respect and appreciation.'

I'd have a personal pity party and yet, the next day when that same person crossed my path, they would act like nothing had happened! They didn't know that they'd cut me to the quick.

Then out of my soul, heart and mind, a voice said,

> **'Ian, they didn't hurt you – you hurt yourself. They didn't tell you the sad story of poor you. You told the sad story to yourself.'**

> 'No – truly?'

> 'Yes – you, you, you.'

What an important moment in my life. I could take charge. I was the maker and the breaker of my emotions. I learned to watch out for the hazard lights flashing in my brain.

Fortunately, this was never a problem between Margaret and me, generally just a handful of people who were close and important to me, but who brought out negative reactions.

Because it only showed its ugly head from time to time, I tended to let it go. But as these blow-ups continued to build little by little, I realised I needed to take hold and sort it out.

I would have a conversation, and all would be going well until I started feeling upset and offended. **I had to realise that I was letting my emotions take control and that they could spoil a great chat.**

I could stop that. I had a choice. It's up to me, not the other person.

Have you ever found yourself in this spot with someone very close to you like your partner, a family member or a close mate? **If you've been suppressing your emotions, they can demand expression, and this can seem to come from nowhere.**

- Hopefully you can be first to realise that this has happened, and help the other person back from the conversational disaster.

- The sooner you sort this out the better.

- Then, you can get on and know what real-deal, down to earth, dinki-di chats are really like.

- We all learn 'good' and 'bad' habits from each other. So I don't want to pass on my 'poor me' stuff to you – but I want you to know that I had to change, and I did.

- I'm the maker or breaker of my emotions – what about you?

Don't let the sun go down …

One of the Big Fella's champions, Paul, said in a letter, **'Do not let the sun go down on your anger'** (Ephesians 4:26 ESV).

This is so important, especially with the person you want to spend the rest of your life with. **This means you've got to get it sorted out before you shut your eyes and go to sleep at night, because when you wake up the next morning it's best to have your heart free and ready to go again in love and conversation.**

There's nothing worse than hurting them and having them turn their back on you. Let's sort it out! Ask the question, 'Can we talk?' Then listen. And win!

How are **your** emotions? You can keep going off course in conversation until you are smashed into **SILENCE or YELLING and you won't even realise what's happening.**

> It is much better to put up the 'time out' sign and ask for more time to think this one through, and maybe resume the subject another day.

You can invite the other person back into the safer part of the conversation with a, 'Let's not go there. That's a diversion and will get us off track and rob us of a great outcome with our conversation.'

Gently bring the other person safely back into the conversation, and you can both move forward. But remember, be real! No patronising or manipulation.

How I changed my ways

While I was blaming the other person for my problem on those few fall-out chats, nothing changed. **Once I realised it was my doing and took control of it, it was a game changer with a super outcome.**

Since I learned these gems, I can keep on track and expect great results. I don't get sucked in like before. I work at taking stock of my words and thoughts so that we can stay in a safe place and space with each other, without any manipulation or hidden agenda.

> You can pick up these points overnight and bit-by-bit bring them into play in every conversation to see life-changing results.

I always thought that it was the other person
who made me get into my little emotional blast off,
but once I realised that I couldn't change the other
person,
I knew I was the one who had to change.

When that happened,
the other person could come with me on the
journey and be safe,
and we could get down to some serious business
for a winning result and get the gold.
Got it? You are OK!

Try this for yourselves. People who previously brought out the worst in you in conversation will pick up sooner or later that you have changed for the better. **Ask, 'Can we talk?' – and then you listen, listen, listen.**

What I'm experiencing now is that they're speaking differently with me. It's so freeing, and it's getting better all the time.

Because of the change in me, they feel more able to have fun in the conversation. They know that they're in a safer place. One day one of them may ask me, 'How come we don't have blow-ups anymore? What's happening?' We can have a good old laugh about it!

I've intentionally repeated things in my little book so that hopefully it will stick for you. Thanks for hanging in there with me.

This is an absolute ripper from the Work Manual: 'As iron sharpens iron so one man sharpens another' (Proverbs 27:17 NIV84). This happens in conversation or having a darn good yarn.

Unresolved issues don't stay down forever so they're going to come out sooner or later, sending you in the direction of SILENCE or ANGER. If you've wondered where all those feelings came from, now you can smash it and get the gold.

TO REMEMBER...

Conversation skills are learnable.

If there's rubbish and hardness in your heart, that's what will come out of your lips.

Is it them ... or is it you?

You can ask for time to think about it.

8. Can we talk about ... turbulence, and really rough seas?

If we have grown up with abuse or turbulence, it can continue to affect us and those we are trying to love, into adulthood.

Wherever you are at, you can have great relationships and great chats. Don't let rough seas rob you of a great outcome. You've just gotta wanna!

Some of us have had a really rough trip in our journey through life so far, and there may be ongoing turbulence. This is incredibly stressful. We never know if – or when – we might crash and burn or get wrecked.

The turbulence might come from inside the relationship where we are trying to have real-deal chats, or it might come from outside – health, or work problems, or finances, or stuff-ups in the world around us.

Don't give up. It's winnable!

Can we talk about ... the spiritual part of the heart?

After a lifetime spent working with men, I can tell you that, deep down, men are spiritual. I've said to many, over many years, 'How would you be if I dropped you in the Indian Ocean in a rubber duckie without a paddle? Would you look up to heaven, or down to hell?'

The other day, a professional sailor came in for a truck driving lesson. He told me about a few of his big professional yacht races in big storms in the Southern Ocean, and he told me that there are no non-believers when you're out there! It's like the old soldiers' saying: 'There are no atheists in the trenches.'

As you can see, there's a spiritual bit to all this for me, and if you've come to a similar point in your life you will know where I'm coming from.

If you haven't considered this yourself, don't switch off, you're OK. Just hit the pause button and get the facts, spiritual and non-spiritual. It's your call.

Wherever you are at, we can tidy this up and you can look forward to great chats. I meet many who have come through to be free to love and everyone wins. I don't mean just romantic love, but in the biblical sense of 'Love your neighbour'. Let's make it happen.

The *Work Manual* says, **'Pray without ceasing'** (1 Thessalonians 5:17 ESV). **In truckies' talk that means 'Keep tuned in with the Big Fella, 24/7'.**

This is good for me because it keeps my heart open and free to love out and love in, to encourage, and not to judge, shame or criticise. That's the big one. Give up the right to get even with anyone.

> I try to make this a necessary part
> of my day-to-day,
> not just some nice soft option.
>
> At any moment
> I go for a silent prayer
> for wisdom or forgiveness,
> or whatever I feel I need at the time.

Let's keep at this most important area of life so that we can gain the ability to have great and fruitful conversations with others – so that they walk away at the end saying,

> 'Wow, how good was that? What a great chat! Never once did I feel left out, scared, or overpowered. I always felt secure to be able to give my best input into the conversation. And we are now charging forward with the best possible ideas and solutions.'

Yes, it's very do-able, bit by bit. Don't try to fix anyone else – fix yourself. Above all, you are OK! You don't have to feel any less than the other person you're talking to – and don't fall for any lies.

Remember, inch-by-inch is a cinch, yard-by-yard is too hard!

Go into every conversation expecting to learn something. Give the other person plenty of opportunity to get into the conversation or the chat or the yarn.

It's no good if it's 'all about me'. It just doesn't work that way.

Come on, you can do it! – ask the question, 'Can we talk?'

If you don't understand the topic of the conversation, just say, 'I need help with this one.' Usually people will go out of their way to tell you all they know, and then the talk can continue.

Let's practise

Knowing what you know now, practise, practise, practise. Listen, listen, listen. Be prepared always to give up the right to get even – that's important!

Just a reminder to consider these points we looked at earlier:

1. **What do I want most out of the situation and conversation?**

2. **What does the other person want?**

3. **How best can we continue to create and maintain the safe, non-judgemental place in this conversation**

where we can walk away at the end with the best outcomes for both of us?

4. Politics, sex and religion can be really touchy areas – and can shut down the conversation after someone makes a biased statement.

At the beginning of the conversation, ask yourself what the other person wants from the chat.

Those closest to you can be the most difficult because of the strong emotional connection. Take note of this point because that's not where we usually expect the problem to be.

There may be hidden agendas, or other matters from within or without have upset them. You cop it for no reason, and you can't understand why. **Remember, there's always more to the story.** Ask the question!

I'll repeat this: There's always more to the story, so stand by and listen, listen, listen. **The 'more' will always come out – just give it time, and then be an aggressive listener.**

Remember, by 'aggressive', I mean: be involved in the conversation. Be alert, interested, and inquisitive. Think about what they're saying and ask questions. Don't take over, though – the conversation must flow both ways.

Winning chats are exciting because **they work. It's not rocket science – it's just connection.**

You can now be the maker or breaker of good conversations. Make it happen!

Getting help from the Big Fella

At the start – or at any point – in a conversation that's likely to be difficult, if both parties are spiritual people, a quick prayer to the Big Fella is the way to go.

Ask for his help to guide our motives and heart through to hearing clearly and making it to the best outcomes.

This not only works for Margaret and me, but in family relationships and business.

God knows our hearts and our motives, and we can leave the consequences up to him. He can always be trusted to break through trivialities.

I'd pray something like this:

> *Dear God,*
> *Thank you that we can talk. Please direct my words the way you want me to say them from my heart,*
> *so that they can be heard the way you want them to be heard by the other person.*
> *Thank you, Lord. Amen.*

It sure helps you sleep with a clear conscience when you know you haven't blasted someone out of the ballpark. I know this works! Stay with it, you will be set for the rest of your life and you will kick goals.

Margaret and I took a bit of time to be confident to talk openly to the Big Fella together, mainly because I wasn't confident that I knew him well enough. **I had to overcome that by asking him to teach me to trust him. It's easy for me to chat with him now.**

Can we talk about ... difficult conversations?

There can be times when the conversation doesn't go anywhere, or it can be difficult. Back in Chapter 4, we talked about some of the potential complications going on in the background. Be aware that you or the other person in the conversation:

- could have another agenda
- could be in a situation where they don't or won't LISTEN
- could be feeling shy, or scared
- could be feeling sorry for themselves
- might want you to share your story – but won't give you theirs
- might want to make it all about themselves
- could be a perfectionist
- could get upset easily
- might have a tantrum to control the action
- might download, but not ask how you're doing yourself
- might find fault with everything
- could be insulting
- could be patronising
- could put you down
- might say, 'I know.' But either they, or you, don't.

If any of these are going on, you need help ASAP. Keep in mind that there's always more to a story and why people act like they do. Get the more!

And if it's you, wake up to yourself! You now know how to have a fair conversation and get back on your game. Enjoy the conversation. You're OK!

Ask the Big Fella for help. Listen, listen, listen. Be prepared to quickly give up the right to get even. Don't try to fix them – fix yourself – and you might be surprised how things start to change.

> I hope you can see that every which way you turn in life
> there's an opportunity to have a conversation.
>
> If you've started life without a lot of help and encouragement to make it happen,
> you can miss out on so much fun and laughter.
>
> Let's make it happen.
>
> We have a choice to make it –
> or break it –
> in conversations.

How many times have you put your big foot in it? Sometimes it happens before you realise what a disaster you may have caused. **Just say sorry if you need to, and make sure you mean it from the bottom of your heart. You're never too old to learn or change!** But you've just gotta wanna! We can knock this out!

We certainly need these chat skills for those closest to our hearts – family, fellow workers and mates. It's always very sad to hear about families where some members haven't spoken to each other for years. Often the split has happened after something fairly insignificant, and it has ended in raised voices, even screaming. Let's fix it! If that applies in your family, ask 'Can we talk?'

We also need the skill to have a great chat with our peers, teacher, pastor, coach or boss. **We might have to live with people we see as 'pains in the neck'. If you can weather the storm, you might get the 'more'.**

There might be a golden business deal waiting for you. To land the cash, it all boils down to what you really want out of any conversation – so think about it and know what you want.

Can we talk about ... trust?

Margaret knows that it's my wish never to offend her in any way because she trusts me. I hope you can build similar trust with your special people – or in fact anyone – even in robust conversations.

- **Start in your heart. Ensure that they don't feel threatened or embarrassed, or that either of you needs to win or lose.**

- Take care in your chats not to do the old 'information download' on the other person or people in the conversation.

- Take care not to make your story too long, and avoid trying to read their minds, just let the chat flow from your hearts.

- Sometimes you may have to take a bullet to help the other person, or people in the group, to gather strength to join in.

- Ensure the other person in the conversation doesn't feel overpowered or 'set up'.

- **No manipulation**.

- You'll soon learn to identify those times that will make or break the chat, so be ready to change your sails for a new direction at any stage. It's worth it.

Smooth seas don't make great sailors

Smooth seas don't make great sailors, so don't be afraid of some rough water from time to time. It brings out the best in you.

Think of what happens to a yacht in a high wind – sometimes you'll need to take cover, but then you can speed ahead.

Smooth conversation could be covering some potentially dangerous undercurrents. Make sure you listen with your heart.

You don't have to drown if you have your life jacket on and you have your rubber duckie. Learning how to have great chats is GOLD – but you've got to have guts to hold steady in rough seas!

If you've been caught off guard or feel that you're having a bomb dropped on you, or if you are temporarily stumped for words and you are not ready to talk – relax, you don't have to rush.

Just say, 'I don't know the answer and I feel confused. I will try to come up with the facts, but I may need time to sleep on it. I'll have to get back to you on this.' Keep your cool.

If you're in a group, just change the subject – it works!

Time and space and talking some more allows the best to come out.

Above all else, remember you are OK. God doesn't make junk!

I'm going to repeat this. You're OK!

The game is not over till it's over, but we don't want to lose it. You have heard this before in this book, but it needs to be taken in. As I've already said, you can lose the fight but still win the war. You may need a little more thinking time. **Have a red-hot talk to the Big Fella. Ask him to show you his way so you can get the best results.**

> The *Work Manual* says, 'His ways and thoughts are always better than yours or mine' (Isaiah 55:8–9, Watto Version). That's why I like to have a cuppa and a chat with him to compare his way to my way and get the winning way.

Can we talk about ... domestic violence?

Our society is increasingly aware of the rise in domestic violence, and the pain men and women are inflicting on each other, even though they may once have been in love. **The triggers might have been there long before they even met.**

The increasing statistics for domestic violence and abuse are sad realities. **It's tragic, and it's wrong, but when we get to the bottom of it, the deep pain and hurt is in our hearts.**

Domestic violence and abuse hurts everyone – men, women and especially children. We all pay a price. The pain continues to grow.

People have to put up their hand and say, 'Enough's enough! How are we going to wipe this out?' If this applies to you, for the sake of your children and grandchildren – give them a clean start.

Our society can be very violent. Unfortunately, many children live in homes where they have experienced domestic violence, passively or otherwise. They react to this in different ways.

If we have grown up with this training ground for life, in later relationships and marriages, the monster can come back to bite us.

If we have grown up with abuse, we have an increased risk of becoming an abuser ourselves. Alternatively, we can again be the victim of abuse – and sometimes an abuser as well.

It's as if an evil seed planted in our childhood bears the bad fruit of violence in us – and the lives of those we are trying to love – in adulthood. **Sowing and reaping are absolutes – so think about the future you are sowing into and creating for yourself and your family.**

As a society, we are frantically trying to find programs to successfully overcome this, but the damage goes very deep.

We can try to cover up an injury, but a bandage only works for a while. There can still be bleeding and infection underneath.

Good advice and moral support are helpful 'bandages' – but really strong medicine is needed.

You have to be prepared to give up the desire to 'get even' – and if you can do that, love and encouragement can help you heal your past injuries.

The only way to true freedom is a spiritual cleanout from the inside out.

This can affect any area of your life – sexual, emotional, spiritual, or financial to name a few! Ask for help from a trusted mate, a professional counsellor, or a community of believers. Ask the Big Fella. **We all need help from time to time.**

If you are hurting or controlling your partner, or being controlled by them, you've got to deal with it now – don't keep sipping the poison, or let it keep fermenting. It will lead to an overdose and the death of the relationship.

Can we talk about ... difficult conversations at work?

In your work situation, these conversation skills still apply. If you feel your boss is trying to railroad you there's no need for you to go underground.

You may need to have a chat with a trusted person or a professional counsellor to help you find a way into a safe place of conversation with your boss.

Or you can let your performance do the talking. Don't try to tell him/her, just show them – and if they're any good, they'll get it!

Also consider time, place and space before you confront the situation. Sometimes your first emotional reaction isn't always the most effective way to deal with it. This can happen anywhere, any time of the day. A little comment that doesn't seem very significant can gain extra weight when made in front of fellow workers, players, or even in a social situation with a group.

If you hurt someone in this way, they may need time to debrief with others, and consider their response before you continue the conversation.

Can we talk about ... shift work and working away from home?

Maybe you're a shift worker, you're in the armed forces, or you're a FIFO worker. This may be because of the specialised kind of work you do, or because it's a way to pay the bills. If you are, it's even harder to have a talk with the special people in your life.

- It can be hard to find time to talk even if you live at home, when you work different hours to the rest of your family.

- If you're away, FaceTime, Skype and email are good, but can't compare with – for instance – being able to give your child a hug if they've won an award, it's their birthday, or they are having a bad day.

- This situation can be deadly. It can kill relationships as well as people, if they find it makes life just too hard.

- It can also be very difficult for your partner while he or she is trying to keep the home and family together, often while working at their own job.

- We need all the help we can find, to get the gold and make it happen – to keep the real-deal love happening forever amidst the many battles.

- We may need to learn all over again how to communicate with those we love most. We've had to learn to live apart, and that can cause friction and frustration.

Barry's story:

While my mate Barry was away at work, his wife and adult daughter got on with their lives, keeping the home fires burning without any problem. When he returned home, Barry's tone and behaviour upset them, and communication broke down completely.

Eventually, his daughter lovingly let him know that when he came home it unsettled the flow of everything that was going along OK.

Poor old Barry didn't even know that living away had toughened him up. He could have thought that his family didn't want him around anymore. Not true! They all came to the realisation that there was a readjustment needed in communication to get back on track.

Barry owned the problem of communication and sorted it out so that he could be right with his wife and daughter. They were all prepared to speak openly and give up the right to get even or score points.

The Big Fella gave Barry's family what they needed, to get back safely into great love and

conversation – plenty of love, appreciation and gratitude for each other without manipulation.

Parents who are often absent, or live elsewhere, can also disrupt their children's behaviour patterns. The parent who's the main caregiver will have established routines that can be totally disrupted when their partner, or ex-partner, indulges the children or has different ways of disciplining them.

So where do we go for help to change? Often we revert to old ways that can hurt those we love.

It takes a lot of courage, and you might be by yourself, far from home. Start with talking to the Big Fella, and look for help wherever it is offered – other family members, friends, your doctor, or a counsellor.

TO REMEMBER...

- We learned how to talk to people in childhood – but we can change it!

- We never stop learning. It can be painful, but it's worth it. No pain, no gain.

- You are the maker or breaker of your own emotions.

- For new and free real-deal love, you need to give up the right to get even.

- Don't go to bed angry. Sort it out.

- Ask for help from the Big Fella!

CAN WE TALK?

9. Can we talk about ... encouraging each other?

This is the most enjoyable part of this book for me. **Encouragement is an absolute must.** This goes for everyone around you.

If you didn't grow up with encouragement, and haven't worked in an encouraging workplace, let's sort it out now!

We all need encouragement!

I'm naturally an encourager, and I can tell you that it's easy to give, receive, and pass on encouragement to others. **It's a teachable skill, and it can change nations.**

Seriously, can anyone get by without it? I don't believe so. I reckon most people receive a minimal amount. This should not, and need not, be the case – it can be changed.

So, how do you get more encouragement? Once you learn to give encouragement, eventually it will come back to you in bucketloads. It's a gift that keeps on giving!

Who would have thought that my saying **'I've never seen anyone go backwards with encouragement'** would have helped so many to become real-deal champions?

It began with my first book, *Every Bloke's a Champion – Even You!* In it, I shared some gold I had picked up on my journey through life.

I now hear that saying all over our country, and people love hearing and saying it. I hope you like it and want to spread it even further! When we're treated like a champion, we start living like one.

No-one misses out on the battle

I say life's a series of battles and no-one misses out. They've just got different names and times. **It's how you handle them that counts.**

Our day-to-day living can be much tougher without any encouragement. It can be mighty tough if we constantly cop judgement, criticism, shaming or the silent treatment.

It's hard to keep getting back up from that, especially from the one we love. Does your partner, or any other close family member, do that to you?

But then, do you do it to them?

My business life was set alight by my treasured mate, big Jonesy, empowering me when I told him I was going to leave my office job and buy a truck. He said, **'Watto, you'll never look back!'** And I haven't. That's all it took to set me alight in business.

Have you ever experienced a word like that? Perhaps you have, but you may have missed it? **Let's help you to be ready for the next turbocharged word of encouragement coming your way.**

Once you know how healthy it is to receive an encouraging word and how it can change your whole being, you'll want to learn how to give encouragement to others so that you can see them charge off onwards and upwards. It's so exciting and the gold starts to happen.

It doesn't take much, just a little word from someone we respect. **Right at this moment, who's in your thoughts or on your mind?** Why not pick up the phone and say, 'Hi. I've been thinking about you. How's it going?'

Then listen carefully and give a kind word of encouragement. I guarantee you'll make that person's day. It may be that the mate you ring might be in a battle of his or her own.

A wonderful promise from the *Work Manual*... and it works!

> Nothing is more appealing
> than speaking beautiful, life-giving words.
> For they release sweetness to our souls,
> and inner healing to our spirits.
> (Proverbs 16:24 TPT)

Have you had people speak the power of words into your heart and spirit? **We all want and need encouragement. It can make us, or the lack of it can break us.**

A person who receives encouragement is like a plant in the garden. Give it the right amount of water and sunshine and it will keep looking better and better. No water, no encouragement – the plant withers and dies. We can be like that. We can get around, but we're like a dead person walking. Encouragement is the most amazing thing.

> It's normal for us all to need an affirming,
> encouraging word,
> no matter how old we are.
> You can give it in so many different ways.
> Think about the personality type of the person
> you're encouraging,
> and try to figure out what will work best for them.

What are some of the things that encourage you? I reckon we could quickly and easily fill a page if we stop and think of the people and things around us. **You'll never see anyone die from over-praise, over-love or over-encouragement.**

A Watto Tip:

Watch the tone of your voice. It can be cruel or kind. Think before you speak. Think and speak from your heart. Try it – it's not hard!

It's all about communication ... can we talk?

Take care – communication isn't always connection. But a great deal of successful real-deal love comes from good communication. In fact, it is the key.

When someone tells you something important, ask them to repeat it. Margaret loves me doing this because she knows she has my full attention.

Usually we listen the first time in our head and have a quick answer or want to rush off to instantly fix the problem. **When we get people to repeat it, we can listen in our heart.**

After that we can get our head and heart together. Out comes the gold, and we keep coming up with great solutions together. Once I got this going with Margaret, we became much closer. She knew that I cared about her thoughts – that's encouragement.

Encouragement makes our hearts go 'ping!'

Everyone needs turbocharged affirming words. We all long to know we're especially loved and cherished. How are you at speaking encouraging words to the special people in your life? Here's some ideas!

- Tell them how much you love them, OFTEN.

- Appreciate them for what they stand for and what they mean to you.

- Keep a recent picture on the screen of your phone.

Get your priorities in order – partner, children, job, then other stuff. Get this out of whack and you pay a price.

If you acknowledge the spiritual part of you, you will put the Big Fella first and include him in everything. This was a big step for me to take, but God gently showed me how to get the gold in love after I put him first – then Margaret.

Take a serious look at this. **If you don't get this order right, the wheels can fall off.** Let's face it, this is one of the hardest things to get right. **I wish I'd learned it sooner.**

Watch out for hurtful, and sometimes killing, words

We can sometimes say things that we think are funny or smart but they might really hurt others, who might feel criticised or even ashamed. I'll list some as a warning for 'danger ahead'.

- **If you criticise or talk down to someone you won't even get real-deal love off the ground.** Be careful if you start making judgements or negative comments about people or things that are important to them. If you're not aware of their particular struggles or special needs, you can be critical or hurtful without realising what you're doing.

- It's possible to make them feel shame. **Don't criticise or try some smart remark in public at the expense of your partner and hope they pick up a hint.** If you have something to say, do so in private – gently. Give praise in public.

- **Don't complain about and criticise your in-laws.** They're part of the package!

- **Don't rubbish your partner's close friends.** They don't have to be your friends. Sometimes this is just the way it is.

- **Don't knock their spirituality if you're not there yet.** That will hurt them heaps and affect your intimacy.

- **If you're the spiritual one – no preaching, no unreal expectations or pushing them into your way of thinking.** They must learn in their own way and time. Love them through your own journey, and your journey together.

Have a serious look at this! **Don't commit spiritual adultery. Don't tell another person deep and meaningful stuff that you haven't yet talked about with your partner.** Once you've done that, if they agree, it's OK to share with others.

If, for instance, you share deep, heart issues with someone who works closely with you, you begin to connect in your heart with them. That hurts your relationship with your partner and hinders their love for you. **A heart connection can lead to more consequences, which can be good or bad – and watch out, the bad bites hard!**

Another area that needs to be looked at in our marriage is showing respect to our partner's parents and family. If you think you're being smart by making fun of them or taking cheap shots, you're not – you're just causing harm.

Most of us have difficult relationships with a parent or someone else in our family. Your partner may be struggling to break free of things in their family and personal history. Be sensitive.

There's a spiritual consequence and blessing, too. **The Work Manual promises 'all' goes well if you honour your ma and pa!** (Exodus 20:12, Deuteronomy 5:16)

If nothing's going well for you at present, pause and have a look at how you are honouring your Mum and Dad – then do something about it. If nothing happens, nothing happens. At any age, you may need to forgive, or say sorry and be forgiven.

Don't be a hypocrite. Cut out the religiosity and church stuff full of rules and have-to's. Don't be Mr or Ms Perfect in church circles on Sundays and someone else in the home for the rest of the week. Be consistent in your behaviour. It's in the home where it counts.

Don't try to pick up someone in the sleazy part of town, or have it off with your friend's partner behind their back. No sexting to a third party.

All these types of things and more can have huge consequences. You will miss real-deal dinky-di love, and connection is soon lost.

Encouragement can take different forms

My mate Bob, who's a retired teacher, told me the following story, which he calls 'The Parable of the Roofing Nail'.

The builder rang. 'Bob, have you forgotten your appointment with the man fitting your screen?' I got there in ten minutes and apologised for being late. The man seemed distressed.

'How are you?' I asked.

'I'm shattered. Haven't slept all night.'

'What happened?'

'I drive a lot in this job. I'm very attentive. Yesterday, a girl was trying to turn right so I flashed the lights and beckoned her through. She planted her foot. At the same time, a motor bike came flying through on the inside. He T-boned her.'

'How awful!'

'I jumped out. He was gone, I was sure of it – his eyes rolled back in his head. I squeezed his hand. "Can you hear me mate?" He opened his eyes. The ambulance came. The police came. I was so distressed, I forgot to ask which hospital. I haven't been able to find him. I feel so guilty.'

'Awful! I hope you can find him,' I said. 'Would you like a coffee? Sounds like you need one.'

'Thanks. Milk and two sugars.'

As I gave him his coffee and a cookie, I said, 'Do you pray?'

'No!' he said. 'I don't do prayer.'

I said, 'I'm a Religious Education teacher. I teach my students who don't really believe, how to express their need and release their pain. Just say what you want out loud and say "let this be!" What were you intending when you let the girl through?'

'Courtesy.'

I said, 'Yes, and generosity. And he is injured, and the girl must be horrified, and you are shattered. What do you need?'

'Forgiveness!'

'I'll say it for you: You are forgiven, you are forgiven, you are forgiven.'

'But I'm such a careful driver,' he said.

'Come with me,' I said and took him to the back deck. 'See this beautiful building full of light? The builders have done a beautiful job with its soaring roof. And there look…a bally great roofing screw sticking through where it shouldn't be. I'm going to leave it there to remind me – bad stuff happens. The Shakers used to make beautiful quilts but always deliberately sewed in a faulty stitch because this world is not perfect.'

We went back and finished our coffee. I offered a prayer, modifying one from Sister Julian for him: 'It's OK, it's OK, it's gonna be OK.'

'This will change you,' I said, 'But good can come out of awful things.'

As he left, he thanked me for the coffee and the talk.

One of my mates and his wife recently lost their only daughter in a car smash. Some years previously they'd lost their son. Can you imagine how wrecked they felt? **I shook his hand, gave him a gentle blokey hand on the shoulder, and encouraged him to talk out his pain and grief as he needed.**

He said that, some days, he just can't move.

We became mates way back, through our interest in race-horses and trying to pick winners from time to time. I don't bother with going to the TAB now, but he does. I told him his daughter would be smiling in heaven if she knew that he occasionally took a treble, and to keep doing stuff that made him feel good.

Gentle encouragement from my heart was what I gave him. **He didn't need a big lecture, or some big story about my woes. All that was needed was an encouraging word.**

A Watto tip: A hug or a hand on the shoulder can be a great encourager. At one father-and-son Shed Night I said, 'If you haven't given your son a man hug and told him you love him in the past week, do it now.' They all sat there and looked at me, and I told them to get over it. A lot of blokes there would have loved that encouraging touch. It's healthy, and we often don't get enough of it.

And don't forget, touch is especially important in your relationship with your partner.

We all prefer to give or get love in different ways. **A woman or man who is 'huggy' and never gets touched is starved.** I'm huggy and Margaret isn't – but this part of our relationship is strong because we know what each other needs. Don't be selfish or ignorant in this area. Just make it happen!

How are you going with this little gem? In the *Work Manual* it says, **'Don't hold back encouragement when it's within your power to give it'** (Proverbs 3:27, Watto Version). **I love this; it's one of my favourites.**

One of my young mates from Shed sent me a little note of encouragement the other day. He wrote, 'Hey Watto, a mate was telling me how well his store is going. He's been promoted to Store Manager. He said the reason is because of this message I'd sent him about encouragement.'

He had applied the message of encouragement to his store and started passing it onto his team. **Because of the encouraging atmosphere in this small store they're getting better sales than ever before.**

The workers 'got it'. They knew that the encouragement they were getting was the real deal. They took it aboard and got the gold.

On the other hand, there's always someone ready to pounce on you if you make a mistake. It doesn't take much to learn discouragement. Just look at the evening news on television and you can be dragged down by all the negativity. Sadly, our politicians seem to think it's their sole purpose to constantly discourage each other.

My solution is to turn off the telly, or only watch shows that build you, not destroy you. There's an old saying, 'Garbage in, garbage out'. Instead, try 'Love in, love and encouragement out.'

What about you?

So let's speak out the gold from our hearts and let the encouragement flow. No 'fluffy duck' patronising stuff, just give out plain, old-fashioned encouragement.

Start with a little word. You don't have to yell it out. Just eyeball the person if you can, and encourage them. Be real.

There are countless opportunities in front of you all the time. You can do it! **Say what you mean and mean what you say.** Especially to your partner and those close to you in your day-to-day circle – they'll glow with love and excitement!

If you live like an island, all alone, and you keep looking inwards, you have no-one to give encouragement to, and there's no-one around to encourage you. We're not built like that. That's not what life's all about.

Even one-liners work well to encourage. Try some of these:

Well done!   Great stuff!   Thanks a lot!
Thanks!   I'm pumped!
Come on, you can do it!   You were great!
You do that well!   Have a crack!
You're a champion!

You make that outfit look great!
That's gold!   You're a winner!
Super-duper!

Encouragement is great to receive. It works wonders for me and I'm sure it does for you too.

I've received words of encouragement from people all around the country after someone has given them a copy of one of my books – *Every Bloke's a Champion ... Even You!*, *Champion Blokes Shed Their Shame*, or *Champion Blokes Learn to Love*.

They've told me how it has helped them sort out some of life's cr*p that has been holding them back. It has helped them on their journey, making a significant difference for the better.

Champions blast off from encouraging words!

It's so encouraging to receive an email, a hand-written card, a letter in the post, a phone call or text, or when I'm at a Shed somewhere and a bloke comes up and thanks me for writing my books.

Who and what lights your fire with encouragement?

Sadly, many people are starved of encouragement – and too often they're not receiving it from the special people in their life. **If you say something encouraging or pay them a compliment, they don't know how to accept it.**

Some people are not used to someone saying something nice to them, especially in a love relationship. They may reply that you're a charmer, or wonder if you want something from them.

This attitude can discourage you from giving them further encouragement, but they need to realise you mean it. **The solution is to give them even more – then watch the wall crumble. Don't give up!**

When you receive encouraging, complimentary words, just say thank you. Believe it, accept it, and get on with it.

If you encourage others, you'll often find you'll receive favour because people respond to genuine encouragement. They're grateful to receive it and want to be around you.

A Watto Tip: Empower those you love!

Don't wait for their funeral to stand up and say some great things about them. Do it today, and empower their life.

A straightforward word from your heart to someone you care about goes straight into their heart. They'll know that you love and care for them. **They can then bite the bullet and move forward.**

Can a hard word be encouraging?

You may think a hard word can be encouraging, but if the person you're speaking to doesn't feel loved and respected by you, your word will be damaging and discouraging. They'll feel they're just being pounded and discouraged.

When I was 20, I was cruising in a happy place, in love with Margaret, and my footy was going great. Then my birthdate came out of the draw for two years' conscription for military service.

When I went through the 12 weeks of basic training it was a major shock, to say the least.

Encouragement! No way! **I was constantly yelled at, abused, bullied and belittled.** Treated like a number, not a person, and stripped of my identity. I felt like a sausage just punched out of the sausage factory. **I felt like I'd done something really bad and they were getting square.**

Maybe if the armed forces had let us know at the start that it was designed to sort people out for the pressure of frontline battle, basic training would have been more acceptable. I understand now what they were doing – in war, a soldier has a rank and number, not a name.

Still, a bit more input would have helped me sort this out. I finished with a king-size chip on my shoulder, and did the bare minimum. **For years I was suspicious and judgemental about anyone misusing a position of authority.**

Compare it to my footy experience: I played from under-12s until I was 24 years old. I had many coaches with different personalities.

Because we were trying to win a game, we always received encouragement from our coach, not abuse. Even his occasional three-quarter-time blast was given in a manner to bring out the best, and not to discourage.

What a shame my military instructors didn't learn how to do that! The army wasn't all bad for me, though – there are plenty of soldiers who show care and concern, and if you asked the question, 'Can we talk?' they would say yes.

If my story hits a chord, take a moment to consider your own place of discouragement. Do you or have you at any time lived in an environment like my military training?

Be encouraged. **You can come from there into a great place of satisfaction and encouragement.** It's up to you! When you're not encouraged it's harder to do your best. **But it's not too late to turn it around.**

Encourage from the heart

Encouragement from the head is good, but whatever courage it may take for you to give it from your heart will result in a win! Gold! Come on, how much does it cost to talk to someone? You can do it. Let the words flow from your heart, especially to your partner.

> Just a friendly nod, or a genuine, 'Good morning', or 'Have a great day!' can lift a person's attitude. We can't get inside their head, so we'll never know what's going on in their life. One word at the right time can really make a difference.

This is a gem from the *Work Manual*: **'And let us consider how we may spur [encourage] one another on toward love and good deeds.** (Hebrews 10:24 NIV) That is, lovingly encourage others to 'extract the digit' and make it happen!

Remember: Encourage, encourage, encourage. We can change the world for the better with this one. It beats criticism, shame and judgement any day of the week.

And remember this one from a few pages ago: **'Do not hold back encouragement from those who deserve it when it is in your power to act'** (Proverbs 3:27 Watto Version). How good is that!

The more we learn to give and receive encouragement, the more we get to experience that place of being satisfied in all areas of our life. Inside your heart and soul, you will be bubbling over with joy.

> **I'm encouraged by the fact that you've got to this point in my book!** I know that your life is going to be more exciting, and richer with the special people you love. You're going to have great and encouraging conversations with all who pass your way.

The power of encouragement

One of the most encouraging things over the last 17 years doing Shed Happens, with blokes all around our country, is to see men who have come from hard times and dirty places emerge open and free and real. They can do this because they come to know who they are, and Whose they are – they've discovered they belong to the Big Fella. They feel renewed.

The proof is in the pudding for them as they get on with their lives. They help put love and encouragement into the lives of others. **They become lifelines of encouragement for those who feel like they are sinking. Gold!**

They don't need any fanfare or pats on the back. They just get on with life, grateful to know the inner joy that comes from the Big Fella. It can carry them through any battles that life may throw at them in the future. **They are carriers of hope, and nation changers for women, children, and other men.**

If you're ready to look at the spiritual part of who you are, add the Big Fella's power, strength and hope to your encouragement. It goes into hearts and souls to meet the deepest needs in others.

It's a fad these days to have a special day for community projects and causes. **I reckon every day should be Encouragement Day. We'd have a fantastic world!**

Look at this little beauty from the *Work Manual*:

> **Be strong and courageous.**
> **Do not be afraid.**

> **God is with you wherever you go.**
> **(Joshua 1:9 Watto Version)**

When we **encourage**, we build **courage into** that person to do something positive in their life. When they encourage us, we're also empowered with courage – so let's make sure we do this with the special people in our lives.

Here's another beauty from the *Work Manual*:

> **Therefore encourage one another and build each**
> **other up, just as in fact you are doing.**
> **(1 Thessalonians 5:11 NIV)**

When anyone asks me, 'How are you going today?' my reply is, 'Bubbling over with joy!' Try this – I guarantee you will get a smile and a positive response. It's a winner!

One of my mates told he'd been thinking about me for the past two days, so he gave me a call. That's a good thing to do when God puts someone on our mind. Ask, 'Can we talk?' and listen, listen, listen – connection is assured. Call them!

We listen, we ask, we encourage, we pray for each other for our needs, and we thank God for what he has provided for us.

It's so good. I try to keep up the coffees, the brekkies, the footy catch-ups. **I need to encourage my buddies, because they encourage me.**

Everyone wins with encouragement. But for real-deal dinky-di love, the stuff that never fails, the first person on your list of people to encourage is your life partner – the others will fit in and flow. You are the maker or breaker of this.

TO REMEMBER

- Encouragement comes more easily to some of us than others, but it's OK, you can learn it.

- Once you learn to give it, eventually it will come back to you in bucketloads.

- No 'fluffy duck' patronising stuff. Start small, and keep it real.

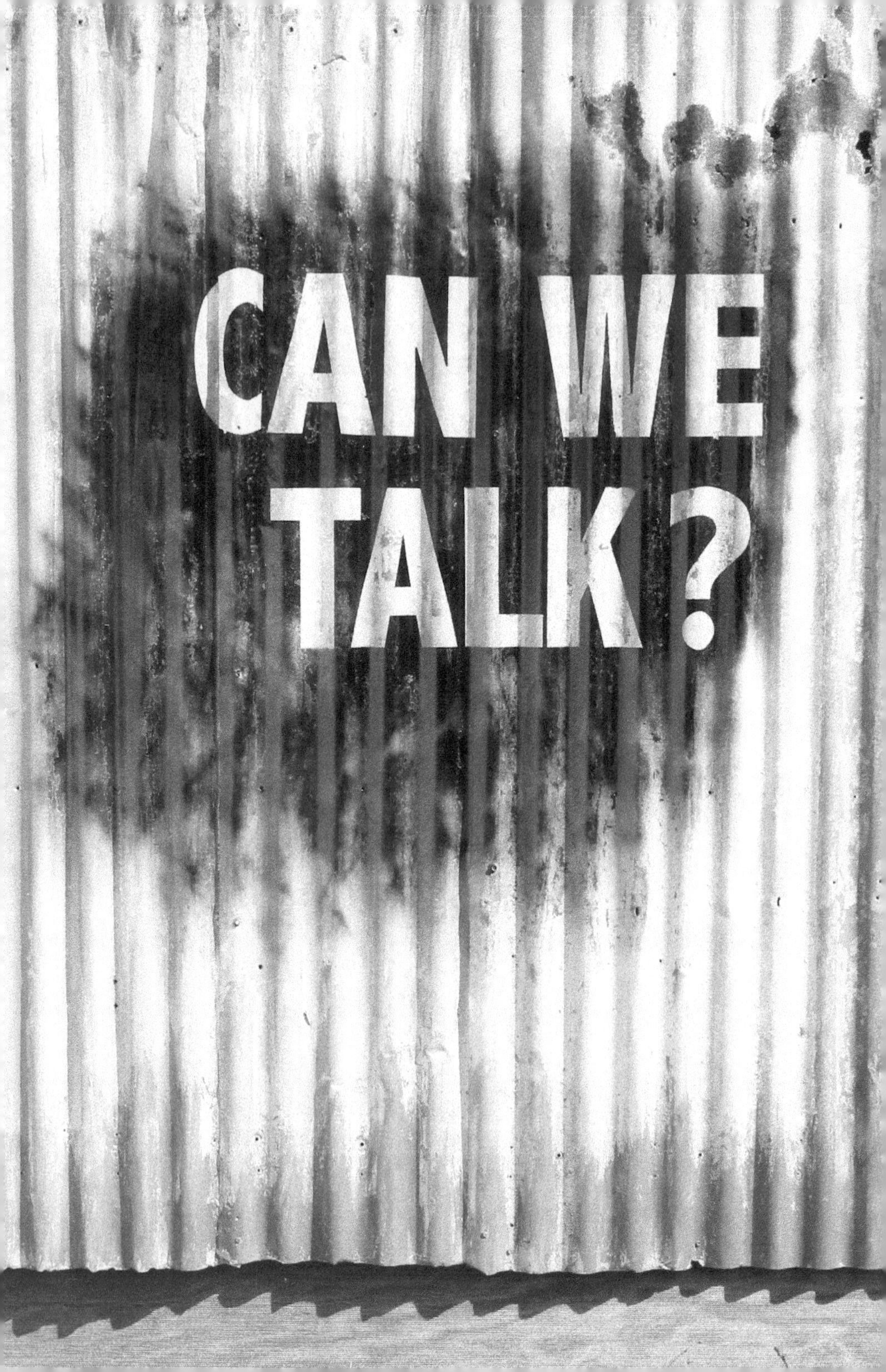
CAN WE
TALK?

10. Can we talk about … sharing the joy?

TO GET YOU STARTED

Did you know that 'joy' is not the same as being happy?

Do you know what it's like to have joy? Would you like to?

Beautiful People, I hope you've enjoyed this journey with me. At the start of this book I asked you some questions. Back at the beginning, I asked you if we could:

- listen?

- hear with our hearts?

- be counted on?

- listen without letting our bias get in the road?

- feel OK to contribute to the mix?

- listen without hammering away with our own opinions?

- encourage another person into a safe, non-judgemental conversation?

- let the quirky aspects of our personalities emerge?

- love the unlovable?

- thankfully take in love and encouragement?

- come to grips with asking the Big Fella to help us learn how to trust him?

On the journey through this book we've addressed these questions, and found that the answer comes down to asking, 'Can we talk?'

To have been in love with Margaret for over 50 years has been my greatest joy, and being a father is not far behind.

Like you, we've had our ups and downs. There have been curves and bumps in the road. We realised the importance of ongoing maintenance – not just for our truck fleet, but for our relationship!

We were always committed to making our marriage work, so when we made mistakes, we could say sorry, say, 'Can we talk?' and listen to each other's hearts and to those around us.

You can create moments of joy in the battle – or you may just need to become more aware of the moments of joy you are already having.

- **Keep it simple.** When I spend time with any of our 6 grandchildren – from the 5-year-old up to the 20-year-old – we can be doing quite simple things together. No matter what we're doing, the connection with them brings joy that flows into my heart and soul. How good is that?

- **Avoid isolation.** If you try to do life without people, you make it very difficult for joy to flow in. Healthy connection with others helps kick anxiety, loneliness and depression. Age doesn't matter – talk to those around you, connect, connect, and listen, LISTEN! **Let the joy flow in so you can let the joy flow out to all those around you.**

- **I choose to do a thing we could call 'right living' to the best of my ability.** That doesn't mean I'm 'always right'! It's doing life the Big Fella's way from the promises in his *Work Manual*, and seeing his Son, Jesus the Bloke, as my true-to-life present-day lifestyle coach.

- **Whether you accept the spiritual part of you is your call. Don't be pushed or rushed either way.** I've discovered that real-deal joy comes from going after God's goodness and ways. You will know by now that I choose to accept the spiritual part of who I am, so I have my heart and soul open to a constant flow of God's joy coming into my being.

- **If you can relate to the spiritual side of things, Go for Gold. Go for God. The** *Work Manual* **is the true heart manual with plenty of gold to help you learn to love and be loved.** It's possible to know the words but not be̅able to sing the songs. We can sit in church, go through the stuff, and not meet Jesus. **Don't get diverted or distracted – just go straight to the top and hang out with the Creator of the universe.**

- **Take what may work for you from this book, give it a crack, re-jig it and/or delete it, reshape it to fit you – and get on with your life**. The best way to get more joy is to keep it flowing out to others. After all, the world needs heaps and heaps of joy.

I reckon everyone who reaches a point of knowing and experiencing the Big Fella's real-deal dinky-di love also knows about the amazing feeling of inner JOY. It's a place of peace and satisfaction amid all circumstances, where God's love reigns over all. It's where the power of love wipes away the love of power.

JOY IS MORE THAN BEING HAPPY. Joy is not just a girl's name! Joy is about knowing the real guts of who we are. Joy is available to every one of us.

Joy replaces bad things and sad times, and the regrets and pain of deep hurts.

I want to finish my book at a place of deep joy. In fact, I want you to know that joy is there for you and me, no matter what battle or challenges we may be facing.

I know who I am and Whose I am. My heart and soul are free and clean. I'm in a great place.

I hope you are too. You'll have a new freedom to be the real YOU and be free of past pain until we meet in heaven.

I am reaching the end of my journey, and it's been a wonderful trip. Over seventy years of living, loving, and learning. Along the way, I've experienced happiness, grief, love, passion, pride, and humility – and much else!

My life changed forever when I let the Big Fella into my head and heart. Psalm 139 says it all for me, and I'd like to share it with you:

> Lord, you know everything there is to know about me.
> You perceive every movement of my heart and soul,
> and you understand my every thought before it even enters my mind.
> You are so intimately aware of me, Lord.
> You read my heart like an open book
> and you know all the words I'm about to speak
> before I even start a sentence!
> You know every step I will take before my journey even begins.
> You've gone into my future to prepare the way,
> and in kindness you follow behind me
> to spare me from the harm of my past.
> With your hand of love upon my life,
> you impart a blessing to me.
> This is just too wonderful, deep, and incomprehensible!
> Your understanding of me brings me wonder and strength.
> Where could I go from your Spirit?

Where could I run and hide from your face?
If I go up to heaven, you're there!
If I go down to the realm of the dead, you're there too!
If I fly with wings into the shining dawn, you're there!
If I fly into the radiant sunset, you're there waiting!
Wherever I go, your hand will guide me;
your strength will empower me.
It's impossible to disappear from you
or to ask the darkness to hide me,
for your presence is everywhere, bringing light into
my night.
There is no such thing as darkness with you.
The night, to you, is as bright as the day;
there's no difference between the two.
You formed my innermost being, shaping my delicate
inside
and my intricate outside,
and wove them all together in my mother's womb.
I thank you, God, for making me so mysteriously
complex!
Everything you do is marvelously breathtaking.
It simply amazes me to think about it!
How thoroughly you know me, Lord!
You even formed every bone in my body
when you created me in the secret place,
carefully, skillfully shaping me[f] from nothing to
something.
You saw who you created me to be before I became
me!

Before I'd ever seen the light of day,
the number of days you planned for me
were already recorded in your book.
Every single moment you are thinking of me!
How precious and wonderful to consider
that you cherish me constantly in your every thought!
O God, your desires toward me are more
than the grains of sand on every shore!
When I awake each morning, you're still with me.
O God, come and slay these bloodthirsty, murderous
men!
For I cry out, "Depart from me, you wicked ones!"
See how they blaspheme your sacred name
and lift up themselves against you, but all in vain!
Lord, can't you see how I despise those who despise
you?
For I grieve when I see them rise up against you.
I have nothing but complete hatred and disgust for
them.
Your enemies shall be my enemies!
God, I invite your searching gaze into my heart.
Examine me through and through;
find out everything that may be hidden within me.
Put me to the test and sift through all my anxious
cares.
See if there is any path of pain I'm walking on,
and lead me back to your glorious, everlasting ways—
the path that brings me back to you.
(Psalm 39:1–18, 23–24 TPT)

Till we meet in Heaven with the Big Fella,

Every Bloke's a Champion... Even You!

IAN 'WATTO' WATSON

'I've never seen a bloke go backwards with encouragement.'

Finances, fatherhood, divorce, depression, anger, broken dreams. The modern male has a lot to contend with. But Watto says every bloke's a champion, even you—and he means it. His straightforward words-from-the-heart help men achieve the turbocharged life they've dreamed of but never thought they could have.

Ian has a wonderful knack for telling it how it is. Andrew Ireland, CEO Sydney Swans football club

This book is for you, champ, whoever and wherever you are.
Phil Smith, ABC Radio 'Weekends with Phil'

This book is written from real life experience in a language the average punter can understand with stories we can relate to.
Paul Morrison, Chaplain, West Coast Eagles football club

Watto will encourage your heart and put a fire in your belly.
Peter Janetzki, Talking Life, Radio 96five

The stuff Watto talks about will help set you free... it did for my husband, and in doing so, has revitalised our marriage.
Julie Oster, Farmer

Pick up Watto's book, have a read and let change begin. Timothy Nagel, Airline Pilot

'Champion, I'd love to meet you at Shed Happens!'

Loves ya guts!

WATTO

the championsguide.com

Champion Blokes 'Shed' Their Shame!

IAN 'WATTO' WATSON

'There's no shame in shame. It has a go at every man, woman and child at some time in our lives. This book is a gutsy, hands-on way to freedom and victory.'

Watto tackles the topic that nobody wants to talk about, but everybody battles with: shame. Painful events in Watto's own childhood created a shame that hung on deep inside and held him back. It took him 50 years to recognise it, and deal with it. Now he wants to help other men kick pain, shame and sadness, and be free in a new way.

In *Champion Blokes 'Shed' Their Shame!*, Watto tells his own and other blokes' real-deal stories of escaping the prison of shame. This book will help men heal from their own mistakes and the mistakes of others, and start living the turbocharged life.

Watto ... goes for the guts of his passion – seeing men free from the rubbish and lies that have held them back from becoming the real deal blokes they were created to be. Paul 'Morro' Morrison, Chaplain, West Coast Eagles

In-your-face honesty with real-life facts and spiritual wisdom that can help you find healing in areas that you didn't even know healing could be found. Dr Fred Gollasch, Teacher, Educator, Mentor and Co-Founder of Better Blokes

shednight.com

Champion Blokes Learn to Love

IAN 'WATTO' WATSON

'Love is such a big word it deserves more than four letters. Let me show you how to turn smashed relationships into good relationships, and good relationships into great relationships!'

We might not talk about it much, but what we really want is love. In *CHAMPION BLOKES LEARN TO LOVE*, Watto shares what he's learned during 50 years of loving Margaret, the girl of his dreams. He tells us in plain language how to build communication, encouragement and joy into real-deal relationships that stand the test of time – not just in marriage but in family, friendships and business too.

Watto gets to the guts of what matters most in the universe and *Champion Blokes Learn to Love* is easily the best book for Aussie men that has been written on this eternally significant subject. Paul Morrison, West Coast Eagles Chaplain, Shed Happens WA

This book is such a practical handbook on how to make your relationship amazing. Dan & Emma Willmann

Watto's advice is easy to apply because these are his real feelings and real thoughts; from a real life that has been lived. Russell Modlin

thechampionsguide.com

Printed in Australia
AUHW011055010819
315413AU00007B/12